T0323594

Cambridge Elements ≡

Elements in Reinventing Capitalism
edited by
Arie Y. Lewin
Duke University
Till Talaulicar
University of Erfurt

THE TRANSFORMATION OF BOEING FROM TECHNOLOGICAL LEADERSHIP TO FINANCIAL ENGINEERING AND DECLINE

Charles McMillan
Schulich School of Business, York University, Toronto

Shaftesbury Road, Cambridge CB2 8EA, United Kingdom

One Liberty Plaza, 20th Floor, New York, NY 10006, USA

477 Williamstown Road, Port Melbourne, VIC 3207, Australia

314–321, 3rd Floor, Plot 3, Splendor Forum, Jasola District Centre, New Delhi – 110025, India

103 Penang Road, #05–06/07, Visioncrest Commercial, Singapore 238467

Cambridge University Press is part of Cambridge University Press & Assessment, a department of the University of Cambridge.

We share the University's mission to contribute to society through the pursuit of education, learning and research at the highest international levels of excellence.

www.cambridge.org
Information on this title: www.cambridge.org/9781009475624

DOI: 10.1017/9781009394734

First published 2024

A catalogue record for this publication is available from the British Library.

ISBN 978-1-009-47562-4 Hardback
ISBN 978-1-009-39472-7 Paperback
ISSN 2634-8950 (online)
ISSN 2634-8942 (print)

The Transformation of Boeing from Technological Leadership to Financial Engineering and Decline

Elements in Reinventing Capitalism

DOI: 10.1017/9781009394734
First published online: July 2024

Charles McMillan
Schulich School of Business, York University, Toronto
Author for correspondence: Charles McMillan, charlesmcmillansgi@gmail.com

Abstract: Organizations rise or fall based on misreading of external signals as well as internal factors – strong or weak management, leadership and governance, proactive or reactive benchmarks of innovation and performance. This Element addresses the commercial aerospace sector with the case study of the Boeing Corporation. Boeing and Airbus illustrate the dynamics of competitive rivalry, and the shifting attention span of senior leaders. Beset by internal dysfunctions, product delays, and certification challenges, Boeing has a negative net worth, and perverse executive incentives, financial engineering values, and governance dysfunctions when confronting the changes facing the main customers, the airline industry. Boeing trails its European rival in market share, R&D investments, and diverse product line based on seat size, pricing, and distance. This case study provides an opportunity to suggest new research directions on governance and managing truly complex organizations.

Keywords: strategic intent, reputation risk, corporate narcissism, duopoly, rivalry trap

ISBNs: 9781009475624 (HB), 9781009394727 (PB), 9781009394734 (OC)
ISSNs: 2634-8950 (online), 2634-8942 (print)

Contents

Preface

> There's one thing that made Boeing really great all the way along. They always understood that they were an engineering-driven company, not a financially driven company. They were always thinking in terms of "What could we build?" not "What does it make sense to build?"
>
> — Jim Collins, *Built To Last*

Rarely do newspaper headlines, academic research papers, and monthly reports of investment analysts agree so closely about the slow decline of Boeing as an iconic aerospace manufacturer. Recent newspaper articles with headlines like "Boeing Ditches Chicago Headquarters for Washington" and "Airbus Retains Crown over Boeing as Biggest Jetliner for Three Years in a Row" are examples. Tellingly, they highlight the internal dysfunctions at Boeing, a company that was once seen as an American engineering marvel and a technical innovator in all aspects of aerospace – including its history as a global export powerhouse, in addition to being the biggest exporter in America, with manufacturing sites in several states, plus factories in Winnipeg, Canada, and Nagoya, Japan.

Boeing's evolution from the time of its founder, William Boeing, reflects the history of modern American capitalism, highlighting the role of private interests and firms who guide the invisible hand. Today's modern global corporation is largely undeterred over time from participation in political events, dealing with government regulation and technological change with a portfolio of management tools, including the raising of capital. Capitalism in advanced countries comes in many forms, including state corporations. In the global growth of the airline transportation sector, original equipment manufacturers (OEMs) of passenger trains, buses, cars, and planes expanded their market reach, accelerated by government measures to promote but also regulate the sector. Today, the airline sector is the main customer for OEMs, with a record of safety and innovation far beyond the expectations of balloonists, hobby fliers, or planes for military purposes (i.e., reconnaissance, armed conflict, and fighting for air supremacy). It follows that aircraft production even from its earliest days has had both a commercial purpose and a defense role, with governments intimately involved as customers, financiers, technology backers, and defense procurers.

Management tools change with the times, and it is no coincidence that the *Harvard Business Review* recently (March–April 2023) published an article entitled "How Chinese Companies Are Reinventing Management" and another one on Western firms learning foreign practice, such as Japanese management innovations in just-in-time production, quality control, and precision engineering. American management innovation coincides with the strength and output of the American economy and the US stock markets, where today 60 percent of the world's public shares are listed. In fact, the rise of conglomerate structures in the USA in the 1960s and 1970s, and the rapid spread of highly diversified corporations in the 1980s and 1990s has a resonance today in calls for fundamental changes in the rules of capitalism and forms of governance.

The rise of publicly listed firms first occurred in Europe, when entrepreneurs saw the stock market as a vehicle to raise money, and investors saw corporate performance and outcomes as a market signal to invest more money or divest. Traditionally, management employed the cash from annual profits to pay dividends but left a portion for new capital expenditures on new growth opportunities. Starting in the mid 1980s, as many firms used mergers and acquisitions to enhance corporate growth, rule changes allowed boards and senior management to pay out excess cash as dividends or use the cash for share buybacks (or share repurchases) or a combination of the two. Starting in 1997, the amount of share buybacks became greater than that of cash dividends. In fact, corporate America recently has spent an unprecedented amount for share buybacks ($1.26 trillion in 2022, see Figure 1).

Boeing's investment policies followed this governance course. Despite its postwar history as an engineering marvel and a pioneer of the jet age with the Boeing 707 and its launch of the Boeing 747, the Queen of the Skies, in 1968, Boeing has paid over $43 billion in share buybacks since 2009, at a rate which accelerated from 2013 onwards. Underneath Boeing's public relations umbrella, high development costs, fewer actual orders than expected, and investors unwilling to invest more, Boeing's state of health was in jeopardy. In Boeing's home state, Washington, posters showing "Boeing Bust" were

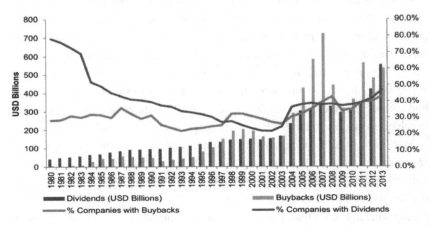

Figure 1 Aggregate dividends and buybacks paid by US firms and percentage of firms with positive dividends and buybacks in the US.

Source: Zeng & Luk (2020).

common. But as the economy recovered and more travel customers took to the air, Boeing rebounded and in the mid 1990s it undertook the largest merger in airline history by acquiring McDonnell Douglas. With its acquisition of the aerospace division from Rockwell, Boeing created a mix of products, factories, and workers in many locations throughout the USA, but the cost of the merger put pressure on the stock price, as investors sought higher returns. Boeing's C-suite and board spent up to $43 billion buying back its own shares, but many analysts worried that it needed this cash hoard to meet increasing competition from a new rival, Airbus. Even more worrisome was Boeing's expensive launch of the new version of the 737, called the MAX.

This Element's case study addresses the evolution of Boeing and the C-suite model of strategy making and core decisions that most firms must address, namely, the pressures from investors and shareholders on trade-offs between short-term returns and long-term growth. The academic debate about boards and senior managers seeking wealth creation via high financial returns and high executive compensation is juxtaposed with a view where firms have multiple stakeholders, a need for a more nuanced view of the trade-offs, including a focus on exploitation of existing assets and exploration of new assets, which influence a culture of learning and innovation. The complexity of commercial airplanes requires huge amounts of engineering expertise and understanding of design issues accompanied by an awareness that even the smallest error can lead to catastrophic consequences. Boeing's design flaws led to two fatal crashes of the 737 MAX, with legal, organizational, and financial consequences that are still undetermined. Lawsuits from airlines that didn't receive orders or who suffered delivery delays are estimated to have cost $8.2 billion, a case of a corporate culture allowing perverse incentives, or penny-wise and pound foolish.

> [F]or a time, Boeing would even become a Wall Street darling, doubling down on stock buybacks that channeled cash to shareholders at the expense of other priorities, such as research and development. From 2013 to 2018, almost 80% of free cash went to buybacks, an innovation in financial engineering.— Peter Robinson

1 Introduction

In the global growth of the airline transportation sector, the OEMs of passenger trains, buses, cars, and planes correspondingly expanded their market reach, accelerated by government measures to deregulate the sector in pricing and entry barriers, starting with the Carter administration in the late 1970s. Airplanes vary in size and type, from small, single-propeller, short-range planes to long-distance jet propulsion. Boeing became the technological pioneer with the 747, a wide-bodied design with more than 400 seats, ideal for long-haul flights. Growth in travel helped the airline industry, but its real competitive strength was with aircraft OEMs like Boeing, Lockheed Martin, and McDonnell Douglas. Starting with transportation reforms in the Carter administration in the late 1970s, American deregulation initiatives vastly reduced entry barriers for both passenger and cargo aircraft and allowed pricing to become a competitive tool. They also accelerated mergers and industry consolidations among smaller airlines, just as more countries began to privatize their national legacy carriers, such as British Airways and Air Canada.

Today, the airline sector is the main customer for the airline manufacturers, or OEMs, and from its earliest days it has had both a commercial purpose and a military role, with governments intimately involved as customers, financiers, technology backers, and weapons procurers. Orville and Wilbur Wright on December 17, 1903, not only made aviation history but also attracted interest worldwide. For 12 seconds the brothers flew their custom-made Flyer 1, made from spruce wood and powered by a new 12 hp four-cylinder engine with a sprocket-and-chain transmission unit that guided two pusher propellers. In 1909, Winston Churchill, then only a British MP and cabinet minister, and later First Lord of the Admiralty in both world wars, spoke before the Committee of Imperial Defense and suggested the Government make contact with Orville Wright "to avail ourselves of his knowledge."

Churchill was an early advocate of air power and recognized its military application, not unlike another navy expert, Admiral Isoroku Yamamoto, who understood how air power could make large navy ships vulnerable in battle. Churchill's restless mindset led him to take flying instructions to get a pilot's license. At the Admiralty, he established the Royal Navy Air Service and the Royal Flying Corps, which evolved to become the Royal Air Force.

A decade before Pearl Harbor, Admiral Isoroku Yamamoto, who was well-traveled (visits to six countries in Europe), knew details about plans by the American and British navies to employ their superiority in the size of their fleets. Other than size, the Japanese Imperial Navy replicated many aspects of the Royal Navy, including ranks and uniforms. In Japan, Yamamoto took charge of the new Aeronautics Department, which planned and developed aerial weapons, including naval aircraft models such as the Mitsubishi A6 M "Zero" fighter, the twin-engine Mitsubishi G4 M bomber, and the Nakajima B5 N torpedo attack plane. Fluent in English, he was an economics student at Harvard from 1919 to 1921. Like many Americans, including William Boeing, a young entrepreneur who made a fortune in his native state of Washington, Yamamoto brought his ambition and gambling instincts to aviation. He also spent time (1925–1927) in Washington as Naval Attaché in the Japanese Embassy and used that position to tour many American states, including the oil fields of Texas, as well as Cuba and its lucrative casinos in Havana. When he returned to Japan, like Churchill, he also took flying lessons. Yamamoto was open to new ideas and less interested in the traditional military concepts of the navy or the army acting alone. He saw how air power linked to other military units – ships, tanks, and ground-based forces – could operate from land bases, attacking naval targets, including aircraft carriers.[1]

In America, the US Army showed renewed interest in air power, where the legacy of the Wright brothers attracted entrepreneurial copycats worldwide, given the centuries-old history of flight, from the first manmade kites and hot air balloons. In 1907, the Board of Ordnance and Fortification and the US Army Signal Corps issued a request for proposal, but the specifications ensured that only the Wright brothers would be the viable bidder. Two years later, the United States acquired its first airplane at a cost of $25,000, plus a bonus of $5,000, because the Wright brothers' biplane exceeded 40 miles per hour. Air mail was a lucrative business, and federal contracts were messy, controversial, and politically charged patronage games. In the 1930s, various initiatives by Congress attempted to strike a balance between established companies, especially Transcontinental and Western Air (TWA) and smaller independent operators relying on income from mail contracts, costing taxpayers about $50 million over four years. The Postmaster General, Walter Folger Brown, held hearings known as "spoils conferences," which reshaped the US commercial air map, dividing the major routes among the four largest carriers (United Aircraft and Transport Corporation, American Airways, Eastern Airways, and TWA).

In 1930, the McNary–Watres Act gave most of the airmail contracts to big, established companies, like American Airways, with the popular war hero Eddie Rickenbacker and a young Thomas Braniff lobbying for the independent airlines. Congress held hearings, and charges of corruption, monopoly, and bribery, mostly unfounded, added to the political rhetoric. President Franklin Roosevelt, first elected in 1932, directed the Postmaster General, James A. Farley, to cancel all airmail contracts and allowed the United States Army Air Service to deliver the mail.

As it turned out, the Army Air Corps was ill-equipped, with inferior machines which were poorly maintained. In fact, after several plane crashes and pilot

---

[1] See Agawa (1969). In one of the great coincidences in industrial design, the Aviation Corps of the Imperial Navy followed the practices of the Royal Air Force by discarding planes with 200 hours in the air. A young engineer thought this was a waste and proposed new design features that would prolong plane life, first to 400 hours, then double that, and then to 1,000. Yamamoto accepted these changes and greatly encouraged this entrepreneurial engineer, Ikichi Honda.

fatalities, deemed by the media as a "fiasco," public outrage forced Congress to take action, and the president suspended the operations of the Air Corps. One of the president's harshest critics was Charles Lindbergh (the first pilot to make a nonstop flight across the Atlantic Ocean), who testified before Congress. The hearings on the so-called Air Mail scandal forced Congress to pass the Air Mail Act of 1934, giving most airmail routes to the airlines but allowing some routes for smaller airlines to promote competition. Regulation was divided among three groups, the Post Office, the Commerce Department, and the Interstate Commerce Commission. Perhaps more importantly, this measure forced a dissolution of aviation holding companies and separated airline firms from aircraft manufacturers.[2]

Wartime put aircraft production at the top of the policy agenda. However, even before the United States joined the war effort after the 1941 attack on Pearl Harbor, President Roosevelt worked with his close ally, General George C. Marshall, on plans to produce 20,000 planes annually. The dour but highly informed Marshall knew that air power alone would need a wider measure of initiatives, like schools to train pilots, technicians to maintain planes, and factories to manufacture ammunition. Roosevelt's views, influenced by Jean Monnet, head of the French government's military purchasing department, led to a proposal for aircraft assembly plants in Canada to supply the French Air Force with parts and components shipped across the border, enough for production of up to 15,000 planes a year. When America declared war, aircraft production was only about 3,000; in 1945, it reached more than 300,000 planes, as factories producing consumer and industrial goods were retooled to meet the military's air-power requirements.

After 1945, OEMs in America had global supremacy in large, commercial airline manufacturing, despite Britain's limited success with its Comet jet airliner. In the Soviet Union,[3] manufacturers like Ilyushin, Tupolev, and Antonov sold planes to the state-owned monopoly airline, Aeroflot, with

---

[2] For background, including the personalities involved, see Black (2003), pp. 320–323.

[3] In the former USSR, three government ministries and agencies, the Ministry of Aviation Industry, the Ministry of Civil Aviation, and the Ministry of Defense, operated a system where plane design was entirely separated from manufacturing, and actual production took place in multiple locations, often near airports. The biggest lacuna in Soviet aircraft technology and manufacturing was not the body frame, which was mostly aluminum that was readily available, but rather the massively high-decibel-count noisy and fuel-guzzling engines, and even the basic avionics, based on semiconductors and electronics. When the USSR imploded in December 1991, some entrepreneurs from Europe and the United States hoped to refurbish Soviet planes with more advanced avionics and western engines, like converting the Tupolev 40 with engines from Cummings, a US manufacturer. Both Boeing and Airbus had a presence in Russia, given the long history of aircraft production there and the opportunity to use Soviet mathematicians and engineers, as well as sales offices. Both companies closed their operations in Russia after the Putin-led invasion of Ukraine. For background, see Clinton (1995) and Hull (2014).

a fleet of 9,700 planes in 1991. Soviet OEMs exported to communist China, third-world countries, Vietnam, and North Korea, and added to the fleet of state-owned Air India. Soviet passenger planes manufactured in Russia and Ukraine never met the technical standards found in the West, including engines, advanced avionics, and the parts and components that make up the final product in the product line of firms like Boeing. Boeing was the pioneer in this new jet age environment.

Today, Boeing has a 100-year legacy in aircraft design and technological innovation,[4] and is the largest American manufacturer of commercial jetliners, with sales to 150 countries. Boeing's design and production of the B-17 (Flying Fortress) and the B-29 (Superfortress)[5] vastly enhanced the firm's critical mass of skills and internal competences in military and commercial aircraft. Two jet-powered aircraft, the B-47 Stratojet and the B-52 Stratofortress, set the stage for a new age of aircraft design. However, after 1945, in the vastly expanding commercial market, Douglas Aircraft Company and Lockheed were the leaders, while Boeing struggled to align its corporate strategy, starting with the idea of redeploying military design for commercial aircraft. For example, its redesigned model, the 377 Stratocruiser, was a market failure, despite export sales to BOAC. Only fifty-six planes were sold. By 1950, Boeing began a series of design tests for a suite of jet planes suitable for the US military and civilian markets (Figure 2).

Cleverly, Boeing wanted to break from its past traditions by assigning the 300 series numbers to its propellor-driven models, so it chose the 700 series numbers for its jets (Boeing's missile division had already adopted the 400–500 and 600 numbers). Five years later, Boeing launched the jet revolution in the airline sector with its 707, adding to its reputation as a design innovator, which dated from its sketches of a swept-wing jet airline in 1949. Jet airliners like Britain's de Havilland Comet and work in Russia gave impetus to a new plane for long-distance flights at high altitudes, with lessons learned from military aircraft like the B-29 Superfortress and the B-47 Stratojet. By 1954, Boeing's new prototype, called the 367-80 (or Dash 80), powered by Pratt &

---

[4] For background on the history and evolution of Boeing from its founding, the period before and after World War II, and the rivalry within the US OEM sector, see Mansfield (1956), Sell (2001) and Serling (1992).

[5] For background on the aviation manufacturing sector and the history of Boeing and its founder, William Boeing, see Mansfield (1956), Stekler 1965), Pattillo (2001), and Useem (2019). In an article in *Fortune*, Useem (2000) offered a prescient view of Boeing: "Boeing has always been less a business than an association of engineers devoted to building amazing flying machines. Sheer technical bravado – and at times an almost willful disregard for financial realties – have defined a company that designed the B-52 in a single weekend, wagered three-fifths of its assets on the 707, and launched the 747 when many observers (including *Fortune*) declared it potentially suicidal."

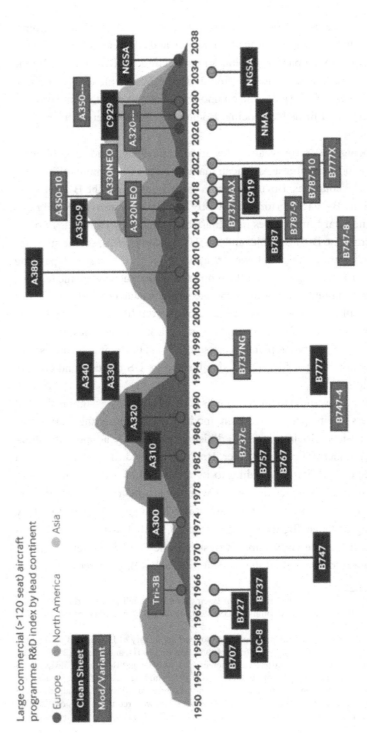

Figure 2 Post-war development of large scale civilian aircraft programs 1950 and future developments.

Source: Adapted From Aerospace Technological Institute Report, 2018.

Whitney turbojets, became the B-52 Stratofortress. Pan-Am was the first customer, buying twenty in the first order, even though Pan-Am also ordered twenty-five aircraft from another new rival, Douglas Aircraft, whose DC-8 was slightly larger and wider than the Boeing 707 (Lombardi, 2008). Over two decades starting in 1958, Boeing produced 1,010 models of the 707 for commercial use and 800 for the military, far exceeding Douglas's sales of 556 DC-8s.

However, the 707 program was never that profitable, despite giving Boeing a technological edge and a clear dominance in long-distance and international flights. In fact, Boeing had a 75 percent market share of all civil jet airliners. Jet aircraft also changed the economies of the airline sector, with the complementary alignment of plane design, advanced manufacturing, and short haul and long-distance flights (including pilots, crews, and navigation tools). Further, aircraft manufacturers, airlines, and airports had government support from the beginning, involving a mix of policy tools like direct ownership, tax policies, and R&D support, subsidies, procurement policies, and other forms of support, such as airport runways, and navigation tools, including weather reports. Aerospace programs today are global, innovative, and immensely complex (Steckler, 1965; Vander Meulen, 1991).

The American government undertook the initial development costs because the US military needed a higher-altitude plane with fuel tankers for its fighter jets. The 707's development costs illustrated the well-known economics of large aircraft production, known as the experience curve of batch production, colloquially known as the 80–20 rule. In practical terms, when a firm received a contract, say for 100 planes, and then another order for 100 planes, the second order would show a decline in costs by 20 percent, and the same for the next contract, another 20 percent, so costs would decline from 100 to 80 percent and so on, but then stop per-unit declining because of high overhead costs. This experience curve effect comes from a cumulative order book and includes learning tools, so this approach to production planning, sometimes called progress cost curves, experience curves, or learning curves, actually dates to American aircraft production during World War II. In the postwar environment, Japanese firms applied this concept with brutal effect against their overseas rivals on products ranging from integrated circuits, color televisions, motorcycles, and auto components, but were hampered in commercial aircraft production by the geopolitics of US–Japan relationships (McMillan, 1985; McGuire, 2007; MacPherson and Pritchard, 2007).

The expansion of the global tourist sector, transforming from a domestic leisure market to a global travel sector, provided opportunities for air travel and the demand for commercial aircraft (Rae, 1968). However, until the late 1960s, the combined assets of the six largest aircraft companies were still smaller than Boeing's. The founding of Airbus Industrie in 1970 as a commercial rival on the global stage was not seen as a direct threat to Boeing's commercial aircraft dominance.[6] Airbus introduced its first commercial plane in 1972, the A-300, adopted by Air France in May 1974; but initial sales were sparse, despite pioneering innovations like composite materials, wing tips, electronic signaling, a two-person cockpit, fly-by-wire controls, and only a two-engine, wide-body design. In the early days of Airbus's entry into the commercial plane sector, Boeing could dismiss this new entrant as another European project to create jobs, and for years failed to appreciate the impact of its new rival until it was too late. Today, Airbus outsells Boeing across the range of models in all key price points – small, medium, and large, long-haul jets – including penetration into America's airline sector.

Long-term success comes from past failures, and high-reliability organizations (HROs) learn from failure, simple, complex, or catastrophic (Starbuck and Hedberg, 2001; McMillan and Overall, 2017). Boeing faced catastrophic failure with the fatal crash of two Boeing 737 MAX planes only months apart – the first by Indonesia's Lion Air in 2018, the second by Ethiopia Airlines in 2019 – causing a total of 346 fatal casualties. In a book exposing the events over several years, *Flying Blind: The 737 Max Tragedy and the Fall of Boeing*, Bloomberg journalist Peter Robison (2019) catalogues the series of errors, misdeeds, and unintended consequences for Boeing, including the grounding of all Boeing 737 MAX planes – those in service, those completed but unsold, and those nearing final assembly. Boeing became the focus of unprecedented scrutiny by governments, pilot unions, investment analysts, Boeing's unions and employees, airlines around the world, the TV and print media, and the traveling public. Financially, it was one of the biggest corporate disasters ever, with Boeing's market capitalization falling by two-thirds, resulting in a balance sheet with a net worth of minus $50 billion,

This Element addresses the organizational and management evolution of the OEM duopoly, the Boeing–Airbus rivalry, the financial and governance practices at Airbus and Boeing, and the new risk profiles as the airline manufacturing business moves into the space age. Boeing's iconic status in America came from the success of its first long-haul, jet-powered model, the 707, which launched the jet age for commercial aircraft, and new models like the 747 launched a new era of long-haul, wide-bodied plane models. The founding of Airbus in the late 1960s was more than just a direct competitive rival. Airbus, slowly at first, helped change the competitive dynamics of aircraft production,

---

[6] For background on the origins of Airbus, see Viardot (2022).

introduced new strategic and ambitious stretch goals, and impacted the geopolitics of this vital sector.

In response, Boeing's response was as much reactive as proactive, more political than technical, in part owing to a series of governance practices affecting the chain of command, such as C-suite executive infighting, the search for CEO succession, and headquarters relocation to Chicago in 1986, before yet another move to Arlington, near Washington, DC. These steps impacted the firm's collective memory system, a compilation of decision repertoires of routines, attention focus, and mental models that determined top-down and bottom-up decision making. The decision to move Boeing's headquarters to Chicago, far away from the assembly plants in Seattle, was an organizational shift of Boeing's organizational culture and added to growing internal inconsistencies between strategic intent and actual execution. The shift was transformational, especially since large institutional investor groups like Vanguard Group, BlackRock, and Newport Trust controlled about 60 percent of total shares outstanding.

Continued financial losses and rising debt raise many questions concerning Boeing's future. Is Boeing a case study of organizational failure in the global aerospace, akin to the once unassailable industry position of General Motors? Are large conglomerate structures still viable when a core product line and technology become a financial burden, especially when the main customer, the airline sector, faces a volatile environment, depending on economic conditions, energy shortages, and price volatility and, as shown by the Covid 19 pandemic, a shutdown in airline traffic? In general, most people keep a nest egg for a rainy day. Boeing, with its faulty decision to spend $43 billion to buy its own shares, led to a cash crisis and an existential threat, from a failure to meet its delivery targets, a reputation risk to its own once famous brand, sale of product lines to forestall insolvency, and then potential bankruptcy.

> Unfortunately, the technological fixes have frequently only enabled those who run the commercial airlines, the general aviation community, and the military to run greater risks in search of increased performance.
> — Charles Perrow, *Normal Accidents: Living with High Risk Technologies*

2 Theoretical Issues in Complex Organizations like Aircraft Production

As the world has shifted to a society of organizations, all aspects of the aviation sector – manufacturing of planes, airports, and airlines – face incredibly complex activities organizations that require hourly and daily interaction, based on weather, consumer demand, and the human desire to travel. This complex system of planes and air transport is one of the safest and lowest-risk human endeavors on the planet. Yet accidents, plane crashes, and the potential of airline failure do exist. The study of corporate strategy in today's hypercompetitive global economy, where technological and knowledge innovation are the norm, requires an interdisciplinary approach and an understanding of how a firm's strategy interacts with existing and potentially new rivals, with implications for customers, suppliers, and new rivals with multiple interactions.

To take a specific example, in less than a generation, the auto sector consisted of highly diversified firms like Mercedes in Germany or General Motors in America, employing the 100-year-old technology of the combustion engine, a mass production system involving a sequence of design, production in large batches, and then a complex distribution system to dealers who actually sold the cars. Today's auto sector is unrecognizable, producing electronic and hybrid vehicles, and new startups from Europe, China, and Japan have a global reach. A leading brand, the Toyota Prius, is a hybrid, and Tesla is ranked number one in America, ahead of the so-called Big Three from Detroit. Autos illustrate this competitive disruption, and a range of sectors, including airlines and aerospace manufacturers, are experimenting with new fuels, like hydrogen, fuel cells, long-life batteries, as well as electricity.

The Boeing–Airbus duopoly is a timely case study for exploring a range of strategic concepts and theories about competition and the internal capabilities, resources, and tools needed to succeed. Constant innovation changes the competitive dynamics in a sector with high government regulation, legal requirements for certification, a complex system of plane certification, and the role, both direct and indirect, of national industrial policies that shape industry performance. Today's commercial aircraft and their manufacture are incredibly complex, with the need to align parts and components into a single, overall system, where even the smallest defect or human error causes collateral damage, even more so if the plane is flying at 40,000 feet. The sequence of construction itself is very complex, involving assembly of up to five million parts and components, and using a modular system of subassemblies to manufacture a family of planes, based on size, weight, capacity, and common aspects like seats, fuel tanks, cockpit and cabin layout, and some elements of avionics.

Commercial aircraft take off and land in airports – almost 20,000 in America alone – in varying weather conditions, and each flight requires a bundling of activities to assure high occupancy, service for customers (food and beverages, potential first aid, and luggage) plus cargo, fuel, passport control, and security clearance. For the OEMs, special skills and capabilities require engineering and human decisions for highly dependable, error-free organizational features, where there is a potential for large-scale risk of danger and even catastrophe. Facing recurrent risk, HROs cultivate organizational tools and incentive structures to recruit well-trained personnel, institutional processes of redundancy and regular feedback, and tightly coupled decision systems. In subsystems like research, design, manufacturing, and assembly, for instance, there are differing forms and times of direct feedback, individual incentives, sequential or mutual forms of dependency and uncertainty, with short-term or long-term horizons.

The pioneering study of truly complex organizations owes much to the prominent Yale University scholar, Charles Perrow and his pioneering work,[7] *Normal Accidents*. Large commercial aircraft production, and related systems like airport navigation and control, illustrate the combination of hardware equipment, software, and human interaction, which operate in real time. Their intricate characteristics, as set out in *Normal Accidents*, include interactions that can display unfamiliar, unplanned, or unexpected sequences and which are not visible or immediately comprehensible. They have design features like branching and feedback loops, but opportunities for failures may occur across subsystem boundaries. The second feature is tight coupling, with time-dependent processes which cannot wait; rigidly ordered processes (as in sequence A must follow B); and only one path to a successful outcome, plus very little slack, thus requiring precise quantities of specific resources – skills, timing, specialized equipment – for successful completion.

Regular feedback and constant learning have become a watchword of HROs. High-reliability organizations often are defined not by the absolute number of errors or defects, but by the organizational mechanisms used to mitigate risks and errors, including redundancy and fail-safe measures embedded into the production system. High-reliability organizations, in short, require organizational characteristics such as high social interaction, expert management skills, and teams that structure activities to assure a corporate culture for safety, reliability, and defect-free underpinnings of decision activities.[8]

In advanced economies, publicly listed firms are assessed by results, usually expressed in financial terms like sales revenues, profitability, rise and fall of share price, and overall market capitalization, and now intellectual capital from R&D investments. In fact, despite a vast empirical literature in economics and business where performance is viewed as a dependent variable,[9] few studies view performance with itself as a different causal variable, where performance itself – high or low – impacts corporate strategy, learning, aspiration levels, and

---

[7] See Perrow (1984) and an updated version published in 1999. For an attempt at a synthesis of Perrow's framework and high-reliability organizations, see Marais et al. (2022).

[8] For background on a growing literature on high-reliability organizations, see Pidgeon and O'Leary (2000), Roberts (1990), and Vaughan (1996) for landmark studies. For a model of organizational failure under differing scenarios, see McMillan and Overall (2017).

[9] For elaboration and a case example, see March and Sutton (2008).

future performance. It is evident that the competitive dynamics of the industry and growth prospects with new technologies can be decisive. For some winning companies, the prospect of immense profits is real. In the United States, for instance, studies show stark changes in the allocation of capital within the firm, especially with the rise of conglomerate corporate firms in multiple industries, technologies, and product lines. More American firms are diversified into unrelated products and technologies, often with a financial arm like GE Capital at General Electric or GMAC at General Motors. Operational risk in executing overall strategy-making can be extraordinarily high.

In response to structural change in these diversified firms, C-suite executives introduced internal measures of rationalization by plant closings, cost-cutting, and offshoring to countries with cheap labor costs, notably China, thus vastly changing the employment and labor market, with consequences like high income inequality. The C-suite increasingly allocated capital with free cash flow for distribution to shareholders, with an ethos of "maximum shareholder value." To quote one study (Lazonick, 2022a, p. 15):[10]

> defining superior corporate performance as ever-higher quarterly earnings per share, companies turned to massive open market stock repurchases to "manage" their own corporate stock prices. Trillions of dollars that could have been spent on investment in productive capabilities in the US economy since the mid-1980s have been used instead to buy back corporate shares for the purpose of manipulating stock prices. In 1997, buybacks first surpassed dividends in the US corporate economy ... these distributions to shareholders came at the expense of rewards to employees in the form of higher pay, superior benefits, and more secure jobs as well as corporate investments in new products and processes.

> America's airlines really do compare badly with foreign ones. European carriers are the best point of reference ... air fares are higher per seat mile in America ... (and) standards of service are worse ... — *The Economist*

3 The Evolution of the Airline Sector

For centuries, flying was an obsession for balloonists, kite flyers, and inspired writers, taking cues from the designs of the ultimate Renaissance man, Leonardo da Vinci. He was proficient in many fields, including mathematics, architecture, astronomy, and botany, so his early designs followed the anatomy of birds – their size, weight, wingspan, movement in high winds, and their capacity to land on a tree or open land. His helicopter model with its aerial screw, a flying machine,

---

[10] In a related paper, Lazonick (2022b) cites a series of American companies in the "dominate-and-distribute" mode, including Boeing Corporation. See also Zeng and Luk (2020) for background on share buybacks in US firms.

and a light hang glider provided lessons that are current even today, including ideas about production from wood, paper, reeds, or taffeta (see Figure 3). Da Vinci's illustrations show the aeronautical changes of a plane's weight, wingspan, length, cargo, and capacity to lift off the ground, and he also understood elements of the scientific method, with its need for trial and error, and the potential for failure.

On December 17, 1903, two brothers in America took flight in their piloted plane called the Flyer 1, with a wingspan of 40 feet, length of nine feet, and a weight of 750 pounds, and powered by a handmade 12 hp cylinder engine. Orville and Wilbur Wright received headline news around the world. This feat started a new form of transportation that would lead billions of customers to fly to distant destinations from their own communities. All aspects of flying would encompass innovation – small and incremental or large and pathbreaking - from clothing and eye protection of pilots to the shift of dual controls for pilot training, to new landing gears by which planes could land on snow or water, to new instrumentation, giving planes and pilots a capacity to fly higher, longer, and with improved benchmarks of safety.

During the following decades, airlines were in their infancy. All planes flew at low altitudes, because weather conditions like high winds, rain, and snow, and air sickness, common even among seasoned pilots, were travel barriers. The arrival

Figure 3 Leonardo Da Vinci's hang glider.
Source: *Encyclopedia Britannica.*

of automobiles in North America and Europe, as well as trains, made air travel an expensive proposition, with fewer than 6,000 passengers in 1929, but over a million a decade later in America. Perhaps the first scheduled commercial flight took place in Florida on the 23-minute run from St. Petersburg to Tampa beginning in 1914, with planes flying at altitudes as low as 50 feet over Tampa Bay. In 1925, the Dutch airline, KLM, flew the 8–12-seater Fokker F.VII, manufactured in Holland, on an inaugural flight from Amsterdam to the Dutch East Indies. In 1927, Pan American introduced its first international flight schedule, from Key West, Florida to Havana, with the same aircraft, the Fokker F.VII.

The history of aviation parallels the story of engineering innovation, whether small and incremental at first, like the deicing tools and fluids needed to prevent ice accumulation on plane wings, or bold and transformative later on, like powerful jet engines or large, double-aisle models for long flights. The entrepreneurial bent of designers, pilots, and financial backers enhanced the innovative atmosphere and culture of their time, a trait that continues in the twenty-first century. Consider the lessons of a key benchmark that took place in Paris almost two decades before the Wright brothers flight in America, when two French flyers, Jacques Charles and Nicolas-Louis Robert, flew their hydrogen balloon to an altitude of 1,800 feet, and traveled more than 22 miles. Daring pilots wanted to fly longer distances, at higher altitudes, including over water. In 1919, two British pilots, John Alcock and Arthur Brown, flew their twin-engine Vickers Vimy, carrying a small amount of mail, across the Atlantic from Newfoundland to Galway, and were awarded a prize by Winston Churchill.

However, more long-distance flying gave concerns to governments who worried about the danger if a plane had engine failure or ran out of fuel. In 1936, the US Bureau of Air Commerce, a precursor of the FAA, introduced a rule known as ETOP, an acronym for *Extended-range Twin-engine Operations Performance Standards*, where aircraft had to fly within 100 miles of the nearest airport. Changes made in 1950 extended the rule to a 90-minute diversion to the nearest airport. The introduction of jet engines allowed Boeing also to change the rule so that jet aircraft could fly across the Atlantic or the Pacific Ocean. Today, air travel has three legs – the planes in the air, the airlines who operate them, and the airports with several passenger terminals, runways, and state-of-the-art navigation systems.

Airline Models and Design

Like oceangoing ships, airplane design and productions require an understanding of the intricate physics of weight, height, distance, and the speed of the plane itself. These engineering challenges required design systems for takeoff and landing at different speeds with a heavy payload in all sorts of weather. Air travel was once short-distance flights, limited mainly to the social and political elite. Today, billions of customers are regular fliers on long-distance flights, thanks to innovations like Boeing's 707, its first commercial jet airplane, launched in 1958.

From the days of the earliest fliers in America, Europe, and Japan, and during trench warfare in World War One, small biplanes and other forms of propeller-driven aircraft were developed and tested. Initially the crew was a single pilot, but later, planes had dual controls for military purposes like reconnaissance and attaching skis to land on snow or water. In the postwar environment after 1918, interest in the technology advances of small airplanes, including production of zeppelins and glider planes, became more advanced. As military establishments built their own planes, entrepreneurs saw the advantages of air travel for speed and distance. In fact, in Europe and Canada, governments established their own national airline carriers, a pattern followed by most countries across the globe. In America, OEMs and airlines led the expansion of air travel, especially when governments issued contracts to deliver the mail – a historic replay of the steady growth of the Cunard Line, started by a Canadian, Samuel Cunard, to transport mail by ships from London and Liverpool to Halifax and Boston in the 1880s.

World War Two had a profound impact on all aspects of aviation technology, from smaller aircraft, like Japan's Zero fighter and British spitfires, to heavy long-range bombers like the Lancaster, to high-speed rockets. In America, firms like Douglas Aircraft designed the famous DC-3, a low-wing, twin-engine aircraft first flown in 1935, and later produced in massive volumes (13,000 by 1945 when production ceased). The DC-3 was easy to fly, could land or take off on a short runway, and had a cruising range of 2,100 miles. The DC-3 saw action in both Europe and the Pacific theatre, and was also licensed to the Soviet Union. The plane was used for transport, paratrooper action, medical aid for wounded troops, and cargo of all descriptions, and was easily adapted in the Normandy invasion to become a flying glider flying at a speed of 290 miles per hour. Many DC-3s are still flying today.

The transition to commercial jet aircraft was a bold financial risk when Boeing took the lead against American rivals like Douglas Aircraft. The 707 became the basis of the firm's jet product suite of fourteen models with five "families" of planes, sharing many design features, like cockpits, landing gear, avionics, and in-service facilities. Before the beginning of the deregulation phase, Boeing's market share expanded with a production of 60–80 planes delivered, plus service work for planes in use with a life span of 25 years. In total, Boeing employed almost 200,000 people, with annual sales steadily climbing to reach $52 billion in 2000 and a market cap of $58 billion.

By the end of the 1960s, America's consumer spending was slowing, in part because the United States was now more enmeshed with troops and air power in the Vietnam War. In Washington, Congress and the White House faced the classic spending choice – guns or butter. As the cost of defense spending climbed, the government in Washington looked for cuts elsewhere. The United States' Supersonic Transport ((SST) program, initiated and funded by the FAA, had an aim to build an aircraft with 2,000 passengers that could fly at Mach 2, twice the speed of sound, on long-distance flights across the United States or across the Atlantic. The manufacture of supersonic aircraft was a technological challenge, requiring advanced materials for the airframe, fuel-efficient engines for high speed, and new forms of avionics and instrumentation. Congress provided research money for firms like Boeing, and the cancelation led to massive work layoffs. Interest in SST high-speed travel came from the very top. President John F. Kennedy had issued a call to land a man on the moon and bring him back, and so he introduced the United States' Supersonic Transport program in 1963, with the Federal Aviation Administration in charge. This initiative prompted firms like Boeing to reconsider their own plans, including feasibility studies of supersonic air transport. Other countries had their own programs, led by a European consortium with the Concorde, and the USSR with the Tupelov Tu-144 program.

The US military remained skeptical, and so did many members of Congress. One senator, William Proxmire from Wisconsin, was an outspoken critic, with a reputation for exposing wasteful military spending, and he opposed supersonic transport as well as space exploration, and called for cuts to NASA (for background, see Brumberg, 1999). When the program was canceled, Boeing and its partners had yet to produce a working prototype. In Seattle, the layoffs – which locals called the Boeing Bust – had severe consequences, with no orders from domestic airlines, and only a few from foreign airlines. Boeing had borrowed a billion dollars to initiate work on the 747 model, but no bankers would provide additional funding. Commitments made to the SST program had drained the firm's cash flow, and layoff costs were high – hourly workers went from 40,000 to 15,000, engineers and scientists from 15,000 to 7,500, office staff from 24,000 to 9,000, plus managerial cuts. Top executives had pay cuts of 25 percent. Unemployment in Seattle soared to 13.8 percent against a national average of 4.5 percent. As house prices fell in value, two real estate agents rented a space on a billboard near the Seattle airport with a telling notice: "Will the last person leaving SEATTLE – Turn out the lights."

However, even before Boeing had taken a leadership position with its suite of commercial jets, the airline industry had its own forum to discuss future planning. Started initially by the CEO of TWA in 1937, a group consisting of the top executives from leading American airlines, OEM manufacturers, and defense contractors and known as the *Conquistadores del Cielo – conquerors of the sky* (Petzengi, 1996). Senior executives met in an all-male gathering at A Bar A Ranch, a 100,000-acre spread in southern Wyoming. It was a fitting name for those in attendance, an informal gathering to relax, spending time on innocuous pastimes like trapshooting, horseback riding, and poker, while feasting on buffalo burgers, prime rib, trout pâté, and smoked bacon.

It was also a secretive gathering, a place to share experiences, propose alliances and mergers, and assess technological advances and government policies. Contrary to public understanding, airlines were never that profitable, and one of the reasons airlines had public ownership was that for social reasons, airlines served small, local communities. In financial circles, there was a running joke: the way to make a million dollars is to start an airline capitalized at $100 million. For executives who crave winning and hate losing, the gathering was a convenient way to collect insights into the future of the aviation industry.

The Paths to Deregulation

Around the world, airlines operate like many capital-intensive utility sectors, for example electricity-generating stations, railroads, telecommunications, the post office, and subways. In America, many utility sectors are privately owned, but government regulation is extensive, particularly on prices. Regulation can take many forms, given public concerns about public safety (airlines and nuclear power plants, or monopoly telecommunications firms), cost (pricing of postal stamps), nationalist policies to force cargo operators to use American workers to ship cargo between American ports (the Jones Act, still in existence), and business cycle issues leading to market fluctuation and price volatility (subsidies for dairy farmers).

The 1970s was a period where market solutions, not government regulation, converged with action to improve airline travel. The academic field of industrial organization came into its own as a subfield of microeconomics, with models like S-C-P (structure, conduct, performance) and the impact of industry regulation on firm performance. A celebrated article by George Stigler (1971), a Nobel laureate at the University of Chicago, entitled "A Theory of Reregulation" sets out the potential of regulatory capture, a process by which leading firms in a sector help formulate terms of the regulatory regime that favor incumbents. A succession of books and papers, informed by data beyond financial issues, such as accidents, takeoff and arrival delays, and canceled flights, focused on the airline sector[11] and

---

[11] For a representative group, see Caves (1962), Levine (1965), Jordan (1970), Keeler (1972), and Douglas and Miller (1974).

provided insights to Congress, led by the forceful leadership of US Senator Ted Kennedy from Massachusetts. The Congressional appointment of a strong deregulation advocate, Alfred Kahn, the new Chairman of the Civil Aeronautics Board (CAB) with government powers to award "certificates of public convenience and necessity," was a signal of massive disruption.

Congress passed the Airline Deregulation Act, which then was signed into law by President Jimmy Carter in October 1978, and it removed CAB authority over fares, entry, and exit. After a short transition, the CAB was sunsetted in December 1984 and approvals for authority over mergers and acquisitions went to the Department of Transport (and since 1989, to the Department of Justice). America was not alone in the deregulating path, but it was the first. Canada, Britain, and some European countries followed, but these countries also deregulated other sectors such as financial services and telecommunications. In Britain, deregulation was a disruptive change for a state-owned airline, where a merger of domestic airline firms, such as British Airways, formed in 1974 from British Overseas Airways Corporation and British European Airways, plus two regional carriers, Cambrian Airways and Northeast Airlines. The impact was dramatic, immediate, and a game changer. Many airline executives had deep misgivings about this new policy, and in America, the only strong advocate was United Airlines.

Three changes quickly followed from deregulation: new startups, horizontal mergers, and consolidations. As many executives of top airlines privately predicted, the ten incumbents (American, Braniff, Continental, Delta, Eastern, Northwest, Pan Am, TWA, United, and Western) lost market share, declining from 87 percent to 75 percent, with new competitive rivalry coming from smaller, regional airlines like Frontier, Ozark, Piedmont, Republic, and US Air; intrastate airlines like Air California, Air Florida, Pacific Southwest, and Southwest; and charter airlines like American Trans-Air (ATA), Capitol Airlines, and World Airways. New airline startups included America West, Jet America, Midway, Midwest Express, Muse, New York Air, and People Express. According to Jordon's (1987) analysis, between 1978 and 1985, the number of airlines using jet aircraft increased from 27 to 62, while Rose and Dahl (1989) saw the second wave increase the number of airlines to 200. (For background, see Goetz and Dempsey, 1989.)

By the end of the 1990s, more competition led to a new period of industry consolidation, with eight airlines having 80 percent market share. Among the bigger players, Braniff, Eastern, and Pan Am ceased operations, and Delta took over Western, leaving a dominant market position for American, Continental, Delta, Northwest, United, and US Air. The third wave coincided with the terrorist attack on the World Trade Center on

September 11, 2001, in which two planes from American Airlines and two from United were highjacked and crashed at the World Trade Center, the Pentagon, and a farmer's field in Pennsylvania. Air travel slowed down precipitously, thus impacting the output of firms like Airbus and Boeing. Terrorism became a new watchword, as airline security around the world meant longer check-in times for boarding, changes to passenger's luggage and carry-on baggage, and careful security alerts by immigration authorities at destinations.

Elsewhere, state-owned airlines like Japan Airlines and Air Canada negotiated new bilateral agreements to fly to foreign countries in a cooperative system known as "Bilateral Air Services Agreements" (BASA). The skies, both domestic and international, were historically controlled by the governments of the world where this system, focusing on safety, was highly regulated, usually limiting the number of flights, their frequencies, and fares, which could be changed only with the approval of governments.

Two other related but separate technology advances impacted the airlines. Since the early 1960s, computer software and large mainframe computers allowed collection, assortment, and assessment of huge amounts of data on flights, new and repeat customers, and regular routes on a daily basis. Cyrus Rowlett "C. R." Smith, CEO of American Airlines, was a pioneering thought leader on new forms of data analytics and data mining, including using computers as a new tool to compile an inventory of seats available for each flight. He began a working relationship with IBM to design an airlines reservation system.[12] Technicians at IBM began work on a system called SABRE (Semi-Automated Business Research Environment), a name conveying a sense of speed and accuracy, with other airlines like Delta and United participating (Copeland and McKenney, 1988). American Airlines was more aggressive, seeing a reservation system as a tool to provide a competitive edge. Other airlines adopted the American SABRE system, which later became more valuable than the company's net worth.

In Europe, a consortium of airlines led by Air France and Lufthansa developed a reservation system called Amadeus, which was quickly adopted by national airlines across the continent. Other reservation systems emerged, such as Worldspan in 1990, based on joint work by Northwest, Delta, and Transworld Airlines. In 1993, Galileo GDS, a reservation system competing with Amadeus, was financed by British Airways, The Netherlands' KLM, and United Airlines. With more personal computers accessing the internet, more

---

[12] For background on the emergence of airline reservation systems, see Copeland and McKenney (1988) and Winston and Morrison (2001).

bookings allowed individual travelers to make their own travel plans, thus vastly reducing the need for travel agents and resulting in a cost savings of about 5 percent for each ticket price. Many airlines upgraded their internal skills and capacities, thus assuring each flight had high high-capacity utilization for passengers and cargo, and better links between estimated demand and pricing tactics, including discounting for flights outside peak hours.

New route structures and global expansion led to another change, alliances among airlines. Perhaps the first occurred in the 1930s when Pan America allied with Panair do Brazil. In 1989, Northwest Airlines, based in Chicago, agreed to a code-sharing agreement with the Netherlands' national carrier, KLM Royal Dutch Airlines, a privately owned carrier but with a 20 percent minority share held by the Dutch government. Code sharing meant each airline could share passenger reservations on either airline. In 1992, when the United States and the Netherlands signed an open skies agreement, the two airlines, not their governments, could decide the number of flights, their arrival and destination points, and pricing strategies. In January 1993, the US government granted this alliance antitrust immunity – a signal for other airlines to follow novel airline alliances.

Star Alliance, founded in May 1997, would become the biggest, starting with five airlines on three continents: United and Air Canada from North America, Scandinavian Airlines and Lufthansa from Europe, and Thai Airways International from Asia. The five stars represented the five founding members with the new slogan, "The Airline Network for Earth." It soon expanded to 720 destinations in 100 countries. Rival alliances quickly emerged, like Oneworld and Skyteam. Mergers and bankruptcies impacted the membership of alliances, but so too did strategic and operational issues, fleet configuration, and cooperative agreements, such as cost-saving measures to share maintenance, refueling, and repairs among the membership carriers.

As more customers booked flights for long distances, each airline had to negotiate agreements with its own government to reach treaty agreements with foreign governments to fly into its territory. For airlines in advanced countries like Europe, Canada, the United States, and Japan, the approach was not a contentious issue. Most Western governments in Europe, North America, and Japan cooperated on many bilateral and multilateral issues, including defense and security, ocean shipping and all aspects of transportation, and trade agreements. Bilateral aviation agreements originated at a meeting in Chicago in 1944, one of several agreements for the postwar settlement, when delegates from fifty-four countries signed a convention or treaty. The Convention on International Civil Aviation, known as the Chicago Convention, set the rules for international operation. Aside from establishing the International Civil Aviation Organization (ICAO), an agency of the United

Nations, it established two rules that guide aviation across the globe.[13] The first, called Freedoms of the Air, determined the right of any nation to determine who could fly over or into a contracting state. When the Soviet Union joined, the Kremlin allowed only certain airlines to fly over its vast land territory, including planes from Soviet-occupied states in Europe, China, Cuba, and North Korea but expressly excluded airplanes from Europe, Canada and the United States, Japan, and South Korea.

More countries joined the ICAO, and these bilateral agreements govern the practices of their airlines for flight schedules, cargo, and all aspects of flight operations, such as frequency, pricing, capacity, and customs arrangements. In time, several countries expanded the bilateral conventions to multilateral arrangements, often becoming part of trade agreements, including open skies agreements, such as the treaty between Canada and the United States. Economic growth and rising discretionary income meant a remarkable increase in the number of passengers, and new business models for low-cost airlines, an increase in the number of routes, and expansion of airport terminals, despite new trade tensions over air space.[14]

However, other factors influenced the airlines sector, including the ever-rising cost of fuel, consumer worries about foreign wars in Iraq and Afghanistan, and the pricing for long-distance tickets. Financial losses rose steadily, reaching an accumulated $35 billion by 2005, and six airlines went into bankruptcy protection. The low-cost carriers thrived, led by Southwest and later Jet Blue, unencumbered by the high-cost structure of legacy incumbents, and remained profitable. For example, in the period from 2009 to 2017, based on financial data from annual reports, net margins of United, Delta, and American averaged 4.6, 5.8, and 2.8 percent, and often negative for some years, while Southwest's net margins averaged 8.4 percent, but much higher for the years 2015–2017, at 11.0, 11.1, and 16.5 percent. They became a model of new startups elsewhere, like Ryan Air and EasyJet in Europe and WestJet in Canada, thereby increasing global seat capacity to 500 million, often concentrated in the peak travel months of summer, December holidays, and school breaks in the spring.

As deregulation became the established policy framework, airlines had to adjust their business models, which in turn impacted Boeing and other OEMs. It

---

[13] For background, see Kasper (1988).

[14] Russia's invasion of Ukraine in 2022 and China's loose alliance with Russia have led to geopolitical tension concerning Russia's airspace. Because of US sanctions policy, Russia refuses to allow US airlines to fly over the country. China and America each allow twelve flights per day between the two countries, but because Chinese airlines can fly over Russia, while American airlines cannot, Chinese airlines have a cost advantage for flights, cargo, and fuel consumption.

took time to see the impact on industry structures, such as the size and number of firms, their product offerings (short-distance and long-haul flights), and the competitive dynamics within national markets. In the United States, American Airlines pioneered a hub-and-spoke model, using smaller planes like the 737 from smaller cities to the main airport in Dallas/Fort Worth in order to fill bigger planes like the 747 for long-distance routes to Europe. American was the first to create loyalty programs, where customers would gain points for future flights. Today, frequent flier programs are standard in the airline sector, and copying is occurring in other sectors like retailers. For each airline, a network of routes is key to their business model, which includes the choice of OEM models to fly (short haul vs. long distance, narrow-bodied or wide-bodied aircraft). In fact, some major airliners don't carry passengers. Instead, they fly cargo, like FedEx's large fleet of over 700 dedicated cargo planes like Airbus's A-380, Boeing's 757, 767, and 777, and smaller aircraft like the Cessna and the French–Italian plane, the ATR-72.

In America, many airlines became complacent, knowing they could raise money in the capital markets to purchase planes, often via leasing. Yet not all investors were impressed, including Berkshire Hathaway's Warren Buffett.[15] However, as many foreign governments began to privatize government-owned airlines despite fierce domestic opposition, legitimate concerns arose about safety, customer service, and foreign ownership. So, governments also strengthened their regulatory authority on issues of direct concern to the public, such as aircraft safety. Further, they also changed their approach to designing, managing, and operating their airports, including using more runways, passenger terminals, and navigation systems. After the 9/11 terrorist attack, airlines outside the United States upgraded their security systems, including items not allowed in carry-on baggage and luggage – guns, firearms, drugs, and certain foods. Major airports around the world set up a trade association in 1991, called the Airports Council International,[16] to learn best practices and exchange policy ideas on safety, environment issues, and security.

---

[15] In his 1991 yearend annual letter, he wrote that there is a "risk that the industry will remain unprofitable for virtually all participants in it, a risk that is far from negligible. The risk is heightened by the fact that the courts have been encouraging bankrupt carriers to continue operating. These carriers can temporarily charge fares that are below the industry's costs because the bankrupts don't incur the capital costs faced by their solvent brethren and because they can fund their losses – and thereby stave off shutdown – by selling off assets. This burn-the-furniture-to-provide-firewood approach to fare-setting by bankrupt carriers contributes to the toppling of previously marginal carriers, creating a domino effect that is perfectly designed to bring the industry to its knees."

[16] The ACI, headquartered in Montreal, is a federation comprising ACI World, ACI Africa, ACI Asia-Pacific, ACI EUROPE, ACI Latin America and the Caribbean, and ACI North America, serving 701 members in 1,933 airports in 183 countries. It works closely with the International

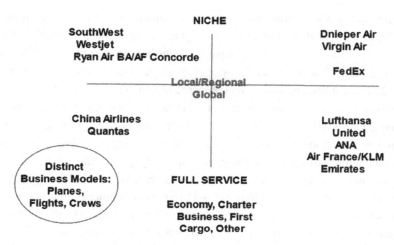

Figure 4 Strategic mapping: business model in the global airline industry.
Source: Author's Analysis.

Novel business models forced the main OEMs, Boeing and Airbus, to reconsider their product-market strategies. Boeing had already opened the door to jet service with its 707, followed soon after by Douglas Aircraft's new model, the DC-8, inaugurated after FAA certification by Delta Airways in September 1959. Boeing's commitment to devoting huge time and resources for the 747 design, with more than double the number of seats of the 707 or DC-8, was a strategic bet on the future, with a large, wide-bodied model carrying more passenger seats and cargo. Rivals quickly followed, like Lockheed Martin's L-1011 Tri-Star, but there were also consequences for airports, which varied by size (number of passengers), location (near built-up areas in major cities), capacity, and international navigation systems (Figure 4).

Ironically, the biggest impact was in Europe, not America, where both airlines and transport policies led to lower fares, more competition, and high levels of service (including other transportation options, like high-speed rail). Deregulation had changed the calculation to manage a fleet for long-haul flights and short-distance, combining high utilization per plane and high occupancy per flight. The emergence of new, low-cost airlines exacerbated management issues for larger companies with larger fleets using wide-bodied aircraft, smaller and more fuel-efficient planes like Boeing's 737 or Airbus's A-319, or even smaller models (fifty to ninety seats) made by Embraer in Brazil and Bombardier in Canada. Measured by performance benchmarks such as fares per seat mile and profits per passenger, America's airline sector remained an oligopoly; despite

---

Air Transport Association (IATA), also headquartered in Montreal, and the Civil Air Navigation Services Organization, with headquarters in Amsterdam.

mergers and consolidation, four airlines accounted for 80 percent domestic market share – with higher fares and higher margins and profitability than Europe, more than double by comparison. Further, despite the deregulatory environment, US laws on foreign ownership remain more restrictive, allowing only 25 percent foreign ownership compared to 49 percent in the EU.

For each airline, a network of routes is key to their business model,[17] which included the choice of OEM models to fly (short haul vs. long-distance, narrow-bodied or wide-bodied aircraft). For each airline, the business model included the calculation[18] of estimated passenger (and cargo) demand, per month and per year, and a sequential series of activities for the airline, the plane manufacturer, and the local airport. In the post–9-11 travel environment, airport security provides more passenger safety, but also more delays (enhanced by the COVID-19 pandemic), thus interrupting route networks, based on arrivals and departures. As International Air Transport Association (IATA) predicted, domestic flights declined by 70 percent and passenger revenue declined by $314 billion once the COVID-19 virus spread worldwide. Airline travel declined precipitously and set off a cascade for fewer delivery orders, fewer production requirements, and less work for subcontractors.

Deregulation accelerated the time for new designs of planes, thus reconfiguring the third leg of the industry, airports. Airports consist of four features: land and real estate, runways, terminals for passengers and cargo, and maintenance facilities, including fuel storage. Airports face new challenges, such as 24/7 security, customs clearance, and facilities for emergency equipment for weather conditions. These factors impact the landing fees and cost per plane. In many cities, airports faced governance challenges, such as the NIMBY problem of local citizens not wanting expansion, with public fears of traffic congestion and high decibel count or noise of jet engines. Revenues come from landing fees charged to airlines, and the rents as a landlord for bars, restaurants, and other amenities. In the end, airlines face a range of costs even when the planes are sitting on the ground, and they asked, as they reconfigured their high-cost fleets, could they afford the capital cost of fleet expansion?

The Sales Commitment and Dawn of Leasing

For airlines in America, whose shares were listed in a public exchange, raising capital to expand their fleets was only one strategic factor in their growth

---

[17] For background, see Johnson (2010) and Teece (2010).

[18] A basic calculation for revenues per kilometer (RPK) is obtained by multiplying the number of revenue passengers carried on each flight by the corresponding flight distance. The resultant figure is equal to the number of kilometers traveled by all passengers: Σ (Passengers carried on Flight A) × distance of Flight A.

strategy, as were new destinations, often to foreign countries. However, for new startups, or legacy government-owned carriers, fleet expansion also presented a strategic challenge – the need to replace aging airplanes, such as the 727, with new planes at a cost of about $150–200 million per plane (and even more if spare engines were included).

In the decade after US deregulation, aircraft production increased to about 392 per year, up from 315, while airlines retired 285 planes per year. Aircraft leasing became a financial tool widely employed by the auto OEMs, such as GM's leasing division, General Motors Acceptance Corporation. The growing airline sector was a novel customer base in the new highly deregulated banking sector and provided aggressive financial service firms like GE Capital and many others an opportunity, often with many tax advantages. It was a new era in global financial services and the dawn of a new asset class, aircraft leasing. Other firms emerged, such as Aerolease International, Polaris Aircraft Leasing, General Electric Capital Corp (GECC), and Guinness Peat Aviation (GPA), which offer airlines an easier form of financing for the full life cycle of each plane model.

The emergence of so many new airlines led to a steady expansion of plane leasing and forced negotiation of a new international agreement, the Cape Town Treaty, which now involves 73 countries including the European Union. The Cape Town Treaty refers to the Convention on International Interests in Mobile Equipment, and its Protocol on Matters Specific to Aircraft Equipment. It established an international registry for airplanes and helicopters, as well as a civil aviation registry as the authorizing entry point for requests to change ownership and to record engines and aircraft as collateral for unsecured payments. (Russia's invasion of Ukraine had many secondary consequences. Many planes operating in Russia with leasing contracts with Western firms became subject to seizure as part of the sanctions package imposed on the Russian government, Russian firms and oligarchs, and their offshore holding companies.)

Starting in the 1980s, leading airlines worked closely for a three-way cooperation of the ecosystem of airports – airline manufacturers, airlines, and airport authorities – plus the flying public to confront the politics of infrastructure, the NIMBY effect against charges of traffic congestion, noise levels, related costs like subway extension, and acquiring more land for new, longer runways – see Figure 5. Often municipalities prefer expansion, with hopes for a multiplier effect on tax revenues, but overstate the benefits and underestimate the costs. Airlines want the extra services of airports, such as more and better runways and equipment for adverse weather conditions, while demanding lower landing fees.

a) **Machiavelli's** Formula	b) **Inverted Darwinism**
(Underestimating Costs) + Overestimating revenues + Undervalued environmental impacts + Overvalued development effects = Project approval	(Max (B/C) at Approval) = Max (benefit shortfall, cost overrun at implementation = Max (size and frequency of disasters) = Survival of the unfittest

Figure 5 Two models addressing the politics of infrastructure like airports.
Source: Flyberg (2005).

In reality, airports and the larger ecosystem organization have grown immensely in most advanced countries. Their sheer complexity based on 24/7 flights and numbers of passengers parallels the technical complexity of the aircraft, and the need to manage so many activities concurrently. These competencies include navigation aids, fuel storage, and weather-related equipment for cold temperatures, with some dedicated to passengers-only, cargo-only, and, rarely, military flights (e.g., Frankfurt in Germany). Yet airline safety worldwide is remarkably high. The number of fatalities per billion passenger miles for automobiles is 7.3 and for train facilities is 0.43, but for airlines only 0.07, with accidents happening on the ground, not in the air.

> If America wishes to close the technology gap with Europe, all she needs to do is erect 51 different sets of customs barriers, tax systems, space and defence programs, science policies, and public buying arrangements: the gap will be gone in a year! — Christopher Layton, *European Advanced Technology*

4 The Boeing and Airbus Duopoly

Duopolies, where two firms dominate a sector, represent a challenge for economists, policymakers, and politicians who face voters' wrath due to bad service, high prices, and lack of health and public safety. The vast literature in academic journals focuses on markets that are oligopolistic (a few firms) and closer to the ideal of perfect competition with many firms.[19] Duopolies provide a test case for

---

[19] For background, see Cohen and Cyert (1965). Most empirical studies of duopoly cover undifferentiated or standardized products which often induce two firms to collude, or accept a leader–follower position, giving rise to a stable equilibrium.

antitrust, collusive behavior, such as setting prices above average costs and using a range of nonprice rivalry activities like advertising, brand building, and others. Well-known duopoly examples include GE and Westinghouse in advanced turbine engines, Kodak and Polaroid in cameras, and Matsushita and Sony in consumer products. Clearly, a duopoly exists in many local markets (two gas stations or two pharmacies, for example), but customers and local governments accept such conditions because their presence shows the limits of small market size.

However, the presence of duopolies in some sectors raises questions about market performance and market structure. The celebrated duopoly case study is the carbonated beverage sector between two American firms, Coca-Cola and PepsiCo Inc. which together control about 75 percent of the market using advertising, product-like extensions, and a focus on demographic segments. A more complicated duopoly is the case of Boeing and Airbus, which dominate the manufacture of commercial planes, with each offering a "family" of models based on price, seat and aisle architecture, overall size and mileage range, and number of engines (Simonson, 1968).

Mainframe aircraft production involves a complex organizational process, similar to other HROs like nuclear power plants, submarines, teaching hospitals, and space aircraft. By definition, HROs operate in a complex internal environment where human, technical, and organizational features interact and where accidents from defects and misjudgments might be expected to occur frequently. Complex and intricate tools of prevention, redundancy, and defect-free quality can help minimize failures, simple or complex, but occasionally can still lead to catastrophic failure. In aircraft production, complications arise from the need for tightly coordinated alignment of different airframes, avionics and guidance systems, and on-board facilities including seating and cargo arrangements. Such alignment requires demanding and precision work procedures undertaken by a very competent and well-trained workforce with more engineers, scientists, and highly skilled technicians.

Today's generation of jet aircraft illustrates the centuries-old lessons gleaned from oceangoing ships. Several socio-technical units work together concurrently, dealing with the body of the plane and its strength and safety at high altitude, plus the stresses of landing and takeoff where the engines and fuel supply have the power to carry a heavy load over vast distances with little chance of a stall; landing and braking equipment to control the plane's takeoff and landing; and technologically sophisticated avionics for pilot control of the plane's multiple functions in threatening weather conditions.

The rivalry between Boeing and Airbus comprises the extent of aerospace supremacy around the world, personal animosity between rival executives, and the divided loyalties of leading subcontractors like engine manufacturers who want to serve both companies (Newhouse, 2007). These competitive dynamics, exacerbated by the long lead times from product design to completed manufacturing and certification, extend to the airlines' demand for certain aircraft models that provide market power to the OEM manufacturers on price, date of delivery, and price discounts for large orders. Both firms also face China–US geopolitical tensions and China's desire to enter the aerospace sector. In some respects, airlines had shifting preferences for certain models, giving these airlines a temporary advantage in serving high-volume routes for passengers and cargo.

For Boeing, which once had a commanding market position, internal dysfunctions and relocation of corporate headquarters twice have tested the firm's competitive position. In 1990, when Airbus announced plans to design an aircraft model of 600 seats or more, the A-380–100, in part because of high congestion at airports like Narita in Tokyo or Heathrow in London, Boeing's tactics took several turns – as a partnership, as a direct rival, but also to thwart Airbus's development project. Thirty years later, Airbus was no longer a publicly supported national champion, or a job-creation subsidy machine decried by many Americans, including those in Congress and US airlines.

Boeing and Airbus and other OEMs like Embraer, Mitsubishi, Bombardier (acquired by Airbus), and China's COMAC, addressing customer demands, have dramatically improved the design systems for each plane model, thanks to the wonders of computer systems (for simulation, forecasting, and stress testing of materials), digitization, and multidisciplinary teams. New models are no longer the effort of the firm's diverse engineering team acting alone. Even small OEMs must apply a collaborative effort with airline customers, leading experts in airports and terminal operations, the regulatory bodies, and financial teams who understand the very long lead times for design, actual production, and the certification process before delivery to the airlines.[20]

Each plane model has a minimum life span of twenty-five years and is designed to meet safety standards of no-risk flight expectations and to fly in adverse weather conditions.[21] Jet-powered aircraft require a manufacturing

---

[20] The time cycle from design-production-certification-launch into service has changed dramatically from a four-year process to a much longer one, actually now extending to seven years or more, shown by the example of Boeing's 787 (2003–2011) or Airbus's A-350 (2005–2015). Further, the certification process for new models, often consisting of over 500,000 parts and components, plus their engines and related issues of fuel tanks, refueling, and gauges and sensors to monitor fuel consumption, now requires intense regulatory scrutiny and on-site inspection across the global marketplace. As a result of this multiyear time frame, managing the actual financial investments (amounting to billions) and the cashflow requirement is very complex, even when assisted by computer modeling and scenario simulations.

[21] Since the 1970s, pilots around the world have had the advantage of flight simulator systems, first designed by CAE of Montreal, where computer technology allows pilots to face a range of potential accidents, from engine failure, lightning striking the aircraft, a shift of load changing

alignment of some five million parts and components and software, for the mainframe body structure, the wings containing fuel tanks, powerful engines, advanced avionics for instrumentation, braking systems, landing gear, and takeoff tools that guide the pilot, and all aspects of fuel, storage, and fuel consumption. The plane cockpit is a technologist's dream – an assembly of dials and mechanisms to control all aspects of the plane on the ground, in the air, and ready to land, and is fitted for all sorts of emergencies, including landing on water.

For Boeing, the 747 jumbo model was a game changer; a reinforcement of the firm's technological edge, it became a movie star, serving as the setting for over 300 films, as well as the model for the US presidential plane, Air Force One. However, as documented in several historical accounts, the 747 was truly a "bet the firm" gamble for the company. The 747 began with some specifications from Pan American Airlines, with a length more than twice the size of the 707 to allow scale effects of lower costs per passenger. The plane's design was revolutionary, with its overall size, its four-engine thrust, and its customized components like the cockpit, the sixteen-wheel landing gear, and the wing span containing the fuel tanks all specifically designed for long-distance flights – New York to Tokyo or Singapore to London. Its sheer scale would require new designs for emergency evacuation doors and chutes, fuel tanks, and powerful engines, for a takeoff weight of 378 tons (833,000 pounds), with an unheard-of range of 4,620 to 6,560 nautical miles (8,560 to 12,150 km).

Airline safety was a concern of both passengers and the airlines, so Boeing engineers and technicians worked on manufacturing tools for reliability, redundancy, and fail-safe mechanisms on everything for landing gears, maintaining flight with an engine failure, and all aspects of the hydraulic systems. New design features also include measures for redundant hydraulic systems, a quadruple main landing gear, and dual control surfaces. The 747 forced Boeing engineers and technicians to introduce novel methodologies and techniques first applied to military aircraft, such as integrated systems for fault-tree analysis to determine where the failure of one part could impact the total system.

Fault-tree analysis (FTA), developed in 1962 at Bell Laboratories and supported financially by the US Air Force, was adopted for intercontinental ballistic missiles and applied by Boeing in its Minuteman missile program in 1963. The system became widespread in civil aviation and other sectors, like nuclear reactors, pharmaceuticals, and civil engineering, which apply failure probability criteria for risk management. By 1970, the FAA had brought in new regulations on air worthiness which adopted failure probability criteria

---

the plane's center of gravity, or even a bomb explosion or a problem in the landing gear, thus allowing pilots and crew to take corrective action. For background, see Allerton (2010).

for aircraft production and certification, and later were extended to air traffic control and the US National Airspace System.

As planning for the 747 was underway, it soon became obvious that existing plants couldn't accommodate the sheer size of the plane. After a feasibility study of fifty locations, Boeing used its own supervisory team to oversee the construction of the Everett plant, one of the world's largest, on a 780-acre plot located near a military base at Paine Field, thirty miles north of Seattle. Boeing's design team, getting constant advice from Pan American Airlines, knew the 747 would be more than a passenger model, so its raised cockpit could allow a forward cargo door for conversion to freighter use. During its lifetime, the Boeing 747 was constantly upgraded and had various combinations – passengers-only, cargo-only, or a combination usually set by the airline customer.

The 1970s started with a downturn in the economy, and at that time many airlines wanted to acquire the 747, with its prestige advantages but need for high seat capacity per flight, just as Boeing's C-suite realized the rising costs of development, and the syndicate of Wall Street bankers was reluctant to increase lending from $1.2 billion to $2 billion, even though it would have a global monopoly. Sales for the 747 were slow in the first few years, as shown in Figure 7. In fact, in the first eighteen months of the initial delivery to Pan Am, only Aer Lingus acquired two planes. One author who followed the making of the 747 was Clive Irving, a British journalist and investigative reporter, who quotes Boeing's president, William Allen, with this telling line: "It was really too large a project for us."

The 1973 OPEC oil embargo was financially devastating for both the OEMs and the airlines, and many of them retreated to shorter flights and smaller aircraft. As Western economies started to recover with demand by the global

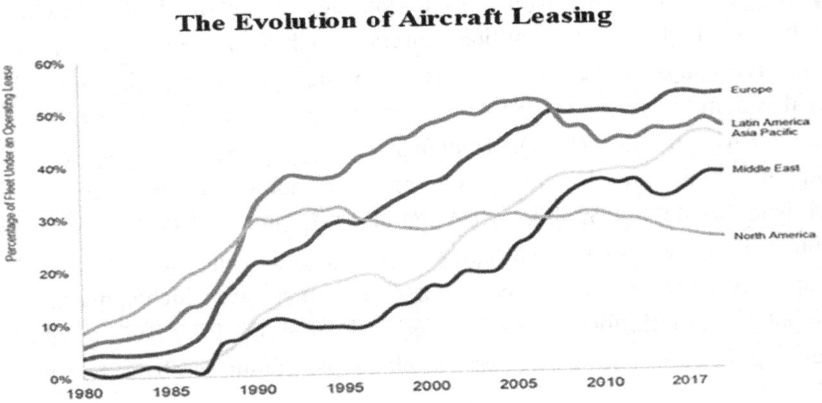

The Evolution of Aircraft Leasing

Figure 6 The evolution of aircraft leasing.

Source: Avolon aerospace leasing.

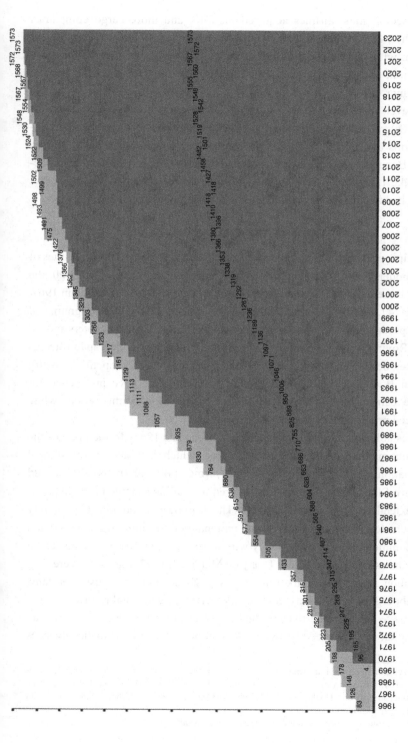

Figure 7 B-747 Cumulative Orders and Deliveries by Year to 2023.

Source: Boeing Annual Report (2023).

tourist sector, most airlines acquired the 747, and more cargo companies added the 747 variation to their fleet. In the end, the 747 was a technological triumph, with variations across the decades providing the impetus for more innovation, and ideas to create new models, like the 767, the 777, and the Dreamliner, the 787.

However, there was one area in which success was hard to achieve: profitability. Overall, compared to many industrial companies, or specialized investment firms like Berkshire Hathaway, run by the "Oracle of Omaha," Warren Buffet, Boeing's net income never reached that of US-based airplane manufacturers like Lockheed Martin, whose net income far exceeded Boeing's. But Boeing had another strategic challenge – the rise of Airbus in Europe.

Airbus: A European Consortia Rival

At the time of Airbus's founding in the late 1960s, Boeing had three families of plane models – the 707 launched in 1958 and reaching sales of 100,000, the smaller three-engine 727, launched in 1962, and the 737, first launched in 1967, plus the 747. Boeing's work with the US government on the SST program, and its new product line with space-age products like Saturn Rocket boosters and the Lunar Roving Vehicle, provided a depository of knowledge capabilities in computer design and flying at very high altitudes. The competitive rivalry between Boeing and Lockheed for the SST contracts gave preference for a plane carrying 250 passengers, with a swing-wing configuration, while Lockheed preferred a fixed delta wing design.

The establishment of Airbus Industrie[22] in the late 1960s formed part of the new thinking in Europe's industrial policy, which included more political coordination, starting notably with two former political rivals, France and Germany. Slowly, this partnership, fostered by leading statemen in both countries, extended to wider cooperation. The European Economic Community (EEC) created a common market, and national policies inhibiting competition and a common external trade policy with other leading advanced countries. In short, when signed as the Rome Treaty on March 23, 1957, Europe was creating a common, tariff-free market among six states (France, West Germany, Luxembourg, Belgium, Italy, and the Netherlands) and quickly brought new members to become the twenty-eight-member European Union.[23] European cooperation was enhanced by two considerations – the US had made advances

---

[22] For background on the European aerospace sector in the post-1945 era, and the early development of Airbus, see Molho and Pleadon (1957), Brooks (1961), Molho and Péladin (1957), Petzinger (1996) and Hochmuth (1974). The MBA case study on Airbus written by Viadot (2022) is also insightful.

[23] For a readable text on the economics of the EU, see Swann (1972).

in new technologies like computers, aviation, and autos (Ford and GM had plants in Europe), and European nations had lost administrative control of their former colonies, many in Africa, but also in Asia.

The origin of Airbus flowed from a meeting of ministers from Britain, France, and Germany in July 1967. The European aircraft sector offered an opportunity to leverage the long history of aircraft manufacturing. Aircraft production was both capital- and labor-intensive, thus requiring bigger markets to lower the unit costs per plane and development costs for new models. The British de Havilland Comet, the first jet plane for commercial flight, cost an estimated £4 million in 1950, and the French Caravelle's cost was 140 million francs, while the Douglas DC-8, more than twice the capacity, cost $200 million. New engines faced the same high investment costs and development time, as did military aircraft and fighter planes.

Fortunately for the launch of Airbus, governments provided a cooperative environment but left the details to the new management team, headed by a Frenchman, Roger Béteille, and a German, Felix Kracht. Béteille was a shrewd choice, for three reasons. First he was an aeronautical engineer educated in French universities like École Polytechnique and at Supaéro, a *grande école* in engineering, founded in 1909 in his native city, Toulouse, with its dedicated aerospace engineering program, rated the best in Europe. Second, he had hands-on business experience, including development work for the French Caravelle program. Third, like many future members of the Airbus management team, he had an open mind, and he cultivated high-level contacts with Air France and Lufthansa, and US airlines, including American, United, and TWA. He decided the language of work at Airbus would be English, all measurements would not be metric, but in Imperial, because airlines in America used it.

Initially, Airbus Industrie started as a grouping of French and German firms, disparaged by the media as a clever job-creation program. However, Airbus expanded to include firms from Britain and Spain, and for years courted an American firm, McDonnell Douglas. Airbus knew it had to streamline the internal decision-making model of the consortia structure, now built around leading firms like DASA, formerly Deutsch Aerospace, and a subsidiary of Daimler; Matra Aerospace from France; BAE Systems, formerly Hawker Sidley from Britain; and CASA, Construcciones Aeronáuticas from Spain. In a strictly legal sense, Airbus was a startup, with a new management team, and had no real experience in design, manufacturing, and marketing of aircraft.

In reality, Airbus was anything but a startup. As a consortium, often used in very big projects like construction, or special cases like NASA, it had a common purpose and a group of highly qualified and experienced subcontractors. From the beginning, Airbus formulated strategic aims: (a) to design a family of aircraft with different seat and cargo capacity, (b) to create internal resources with a global reach, including the US market, and (c) to be the innovative leader in aircraft design. Airbus knew well the legacy of European aircraft design and production, often from wartime needs, and each national company designed aircraft in countries as diverse as Sweden, France, Britain, Germany, Spain, Italy, Czechoslovakia, and Poland.

Airbus received formal approval to launch a new model, the A300, a twin-engine wide-body aircraft. The announcement was propitious, when two ministers, Jean Chamant, France's Minister of Transport, and Karl Schiller, the German Minister of Economics, signed an agreement at the Le Bourget air show (now called the Paris Airshow, the world's biggest), and the world's media were seeking out the inner secrets of aviation news. Boeing displayed the 747, arriving nonstop from Seattle to Paris. The Americans were never shy about their showmen skills, shown by the appearance of the command module, Apollo 8, and the astronauts who would fly Apollo 9. But equal attention went to a new plane on the tarmac, the supersonic British–French Concorde, flying its maiden flight Le Bourget.

While the perception of American superiority[24] in aircraft design and production was universal, fostered by the US press corps, the idea of closer industrial cooperation in Europe came to the fore with the Concorde, initially a French–Anglo partnership. It extended to firms like British Aerospace and Aérospatiale for the airframe, Rolls-Royce and France's SNECMA (Société Nationale d'Étude et de Construction de Moteurs d'Aviation) to develop the jet engines, with a cruising speed of 1,354 miles per hour, more than twice the speed of sound. Only fourteen planes were built, and despite financial losses, the Concorde was a technological triumph, underestimated by its American rivals, with its unique delta-wing design, and a foretaste that a new rival was emerging, with a legacy of innovation for a continent without access to raw materials.

Airbus's Early Organizational Design

As noted, Airbus started as a consortium and reflects the product diversification of a suite of commercial aircraft, but also defense and space activities. The

---

[24] In the postwar period, governments of both parties in Washington fostered a national innovation system, including high investments in the National Science Foundation, the National Institutes for Health, the Advanced Research Agency in the Pentagon (later called DARPA, serving in "beyond the horizon" research, a form of a government venture capitalist fund, national laboratories, and grants to research universities, including twelve technology research universities like MIT and Cal Tech. NASE added to the research output, where America outspent other countries on R&D/GNP.

consolidation of the European aerospace industry[25] and the original formation of the Airbus Industrie GIE consortium in 1970 were part of the postwar transformation of Europe, with a universal desire to extinguish old political and military rivalries for 400 years of military conflict. The timing was prescient, and a new partnership between France and Germany was led by remarkably forward-looking political leaders. With time and effort, the consortium model evolved to a holding company and was listed on the Paris, Frankfurt, and Barcelona stock exchanges. From the beginning, the founding partners, their governments, and senior management understood their corporate mission and governance approach would evolve, thus providing a clear decision flow on both strategic issues and operating tactics. More bluntly, Airbus directors and its C-suite wanted Airbus to be a global player, not a European firm focusing on European airlines.

Three decades later, in 2000, a new firm, the European Aeronautic Defence and Space Company (EADS) NV, was established, renamed as Airbus Group NV, and acquired BAE's 20 percent ownership of Airbus; it also consisted of subsidiaries of many European firms in security and space products. In addition, EADS took 100 percent ownership of Eurocopter SA, founded in 1992, and 80 percent ownership of Airbus Industrie GIE, which became a public company known as Airbus SAS. Airbus adopted a growth strategy and an export focus from the beginning. In this new global duopoly, Airbus had two unique advantages that would later strengthen the firm's competitive advantage against its main American rival, Boeing, with its headquarters in Seattle. The first was a lean manufacturing facility at Toulouse, France, where parts and components and subassemblies – wings produced in Britain, the subassemblies for the tail in Spain, with 20 percent of the parts and components produced in America – were transported by ships, barges, and air for final assembly. The Toulouse factory was replicated in other locations like Hamburg and, more recently, in Mobile, Alabama.

The second advantage was a unique technology software called the "fly-by-wire" computer system that replaced the mechanical feature linking the pilot directly through cables and pulleys with the flight control system for all steps for takeoff, landing, and cruise control. In essence, the Airbus's fly-by-wire system

---

[25] In the late 1960s and 1970s, Europe's corporate elite were well aware that the four main economies – France, Germany, Italy, and the UK – were a fraction of the large, continental market of America with 300 million consumers. This key issue was widely known in corporate circles and the publication in 1967 of a provocative polemic, Jean-Jacque Servan-Scheiber's *Le Défi Américain* (The American Challenge), with its provocative first line: "Fifteen years from now, the world's third greatest industrial power, just after the United States and Russia, may not be Europe, but American industry in Europe." Like many journalists at the time, the author vastly overestimated the growth prospects of Russia and the USSR and its satellite states in Eastern Europe and underestimated the strength of European multinationals. For a detailed analysis of this period, see Hymer and Rowthorn (1970).

allows the pilot to make an input as an electrical signal into the Sidestick; this signal is passed to a flight control computer which decides on appropriate controls, so the pilot does not directly control the plane. This software allows a computer to monitor all aspects of the flight and guides the pilot for the appropriate steps. Today, some Boeing aircraft use a similar system (e.g., the 787 Dreamliner), and research now employs powerful software, including artificial intelligence (AI) and cloud computing, to design and test autonomous cars, buses, and trucks.

Airbus studied, duplicated, and adapted organizational features of US aerospace manufacturers. Load engineers, for instance, set up task forces to design, assess, and test load and capacity factors for each flight; structural engineers worked on sustaining optimum asset utilization of passengers and cargo, including during takeoff and landing; and operability engineers and industrial architects addressed actual manufacture and assembly tools, techniques, and processes, collaborating with costing experts in accounting to apply design-to-cost features in the assembly flow. Thanks to technical advances, a digital model over all aspects of the component parts allowed study at the design and testing stages, plus assessments for maintenance once the plane is in services. Using these powerful tools, Airbus called its system Model-Based Systems Engineering (MBSE), to ensure a consistent and traceable link from design mission to operations execution, and engineering tools to future airplane models.

Slowly, Airbus was becoming an established corporate brand, despite initial sales mainly to European airlines. Plans to design a suite of airplane models of varying seat size, and models for passengers, cargo, and military models, enhanced the focus on developing competences and capabilities with a modular design production system. Airbus also focused on the complicated ecosystem across member countries and independent suppliers like the engine firms (mainly Rolls Royce, Pratt & Whitney, and GE). Further, Airbus overcame the disadvantages of dispersed production of subassemblies, with innovative logistics tools to bring parts, components, and subassemblies for final assembly in Toulouse. However, Airbus production plans in 1970 were timely and laid the groundwork for future manufacturing in modular design.

Production systems as an academic field were in flux, as more scientific work in postwar production planning systems began applying tools[26] of operations

---

[26] There is now a huge literature on the changes in production systems, including the human interface between Human decision-making and Machine (technical) systems. A prescient comment from a prominent academic is telling: "From a technological point of view, issues of the future ... include over-centralization, decisions that are too complex and important to be left to single individuals, new capabilities that are so inherently dangerous that they be disastrously abused, too rapid or cataclysmic a process of change for smooth adjustment ... ." See Wills (1972).

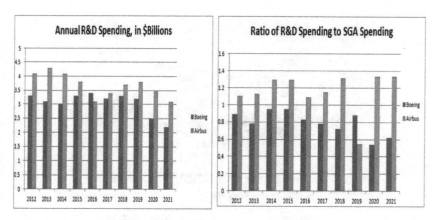

Figure 8 R&D spending: Airbus versus Boeing.
Source: Adapted from Rich Smith, How Airbus will Beat Boeing, *Motley Fool*, April 28, 2022.

research, technological forecasting, software programming, and management science, designed to optimize output. With new computer applications, engineers could better calculate estimated demand forecasts, inventory levels, average costs, timing, and scheduling, with finished output. As one prominent study noted,[27] the production function is "a relation between factors of production and their corresponding outputs determined by physical conditions with the firm. Maximization of profit is accomplished by determining the optimal mix of outputs (products) and inputs (factors), i.e., the equilibrium position."

A constant worry in the Airbus C-suite was the linkages between estimates and actual production output, measured in monthly orders and deliveries, and the breakeven point, recognizing how steep ramp-up and compound annual growth rates impact growth rate of passenger traffic measured in RPK – revenues passengers per kilometer. From the beginning, senior management also placed an emphasis on spending on research and development, knowing Boeing's legacy of patents across all aspects of plane design, manufacturing, and energy, including technical aspects of navigation, batteries and auxiliary power, composites, fuel sensors, and a full range of safety concerns. By 2012, Airbus's commitment to R&D spending actually exceeded spending by Boeing (Figure 8). Airbus also outstripped Boeing in the number of new patents.[28]

Airbus JIT Production System

From the beginning, Airbus understood the challenges of manufacturing commercial planes, the challenges of sourcing from four countries, and the

---

[27] Cyert and March (1963).   [28] Beaugency et al. (2015).

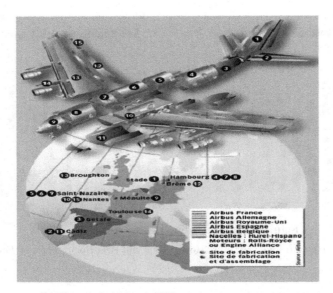

Figure 9 Airbus's JIT production system.

Source: Airbus.

need to be cost-effective while maintaining and improving the quality standards of parts, components, and subassemblies (Figure 9). The firm set up a new Operational Excellence Center of Competence to ensure "best in class" industrial standards[29] and used the Toyota Production System as the benchmark for operational excellence. Toyota's lean production system is actually a corporate philosophy, involving an approach with strategic and organization-wide collaboration with suppliers, a kaizen culture for continuous improvements, including zero-defect targets and eliminating waste. It is also an intense focus on workers, their recruitment, and continuous training, and giving them tools that empower them, thus removing tasks that are routine, dangerous, noisy, or impair vision, often by substituting manual work with robots (for comparisons of traditional manufacturing and just-in time, see Appendix A-6).

The novel system dates from the 1950s, and it applied ideas from mass assembly, but made significant improvements to reduce or eliminate inventory, overproduction, delays, transport bottlenecks, unnecessary processes, and waste. Such a system requires technical training and constant improvement, or in Japanese, a *kaizen* culture. It also demands high levels of educating and motivating the production and maintenance workers in total quality management. In

---

[29] See Viardot (2022).

short, lean production is a corporate philosophy that impacts all existing and new products, using its own consulting company to enhance best practices.[30]

Before actual production began, Airbus embraced just-in-time principles, focusing on applying the system to its unique circumstances – a consortium of partnerships – and the delivery of parts and components to its final assembly plant in Toulouse. This period was an era of profound changes in manufacturing, aided by computer software, novel roles played by subsuppliers and contractors with specialized knowledge and competences, and challenges to the limits of vertical integration and traditional mass production. Aircraft manufacturing is an extremely complex process, and requires a multistakeholder approach, including principles of modular design architecture and mass customization principles. As one study noted (Buergin et al., 2018), addressing Airbus production:

> Offering the service of JIT Specification and thus a high degree of flexibility to the customer selecting each module just in time regarding its module lead time, uncertainty remains regarding options other than long lead time options when assignment step 1 takes place . . . . In this manner, the OEM's production planning department can consider probabilities for option selections when assigning orders to locations and months for assembly. Considering a standard lead time for the time period from start of final assembly to delivery, the customers can be informed about the delivery month of their orders.
>
> In case of the Airbus A320 family, orders can be assigned to four facilities for final assembly: Hamburg, Toulouse, Tianjin, and Mobile. The respective planning task of global order assignment minimizes costs for the supply and assembly of selected options as well as workload deviations. It also considers the confirmed delivery quarter.

Just-In-Time architecture is flexible and allows more product variety at lower cost than traditional mass assembly configurations. As Buergin et al. (2018) emphasize, "this complexity requires the management of several product variants in the same product architecture but also the splitting of this product architecture into a set of elementary items to easily handle the configuration of demand solutions. This decomposition should also allow the reference of the product structure (design solution) to the production process (manufacturing solution) to support the impact of any modification of the product structure on the final assembly process . . . the customers' requests influence the customization of the aircraft and the subsequent allocation of the orders within the

---

[30] For background on how Toyota uses its multiple plants in different countries as a network design system, see Dyer and Nobeoka (2000). Today, to cite an example, Toyota exchanges workers, supervisors, and plant managers from operations in Mexico, the US, and Canada to assure the highest standards of best practices, including systems for quality leading to operational excellence. For background history on Airbus, see Hayward (1994) and Hamilton (2021).

production network. This can be managed as a customer-driven co-evolution of the product structure and production strategy."

For Airbus, the production system requires extraordinary levels of quality and precision engineering, using trained workers and technicians at each stage. Due to the nature of engineering design and to the potential for defects, either in the part or component sent from a supplier, or to actual fittings and factory assembly, organizations need systems to detect errors and apply learning tools in limiting defects – the ideal of a zero tolerance of lean production. In airplane manufacturers, like other high-reliability organizations, each part and component have a multiplicative production relationship with a high threshold of proficiency. The example of the O-ring defect[31] in the ill-fated *Challenger* spacecraft disaster is instructive.

Because most manufacturing involves a sequential process, where parts and components are added in an orderly, scheduled way, a defect in only one part may cause a defect in the entire subassembly. In the case of the *Challenger* space shuttle, one part, the O-ring, was defective and caused the explosion. However, just-in-time processes and management systems demand other features – human resource processes of upgrading skills and high levels of training, as well as state-of-the-art automation tools, robotics, and high maintenance to gain the full competitive advantages of lean production.

As the family of Airbus models grew, Airbus could assign customer orders to four final assembly plants in Toulouse and Hamburg in Europe, Tianjin in China, and Mobile in America, thus optimizing the final assembly for parts and components of the customer options for each order and obtaining better estimates for final delivery.

With so many parts and components needed to align for final assembly, Airbus became an early pioneer combining modular design[32] with JIT manufacturing, starting with the A-319. Sourcing large subassemblies was a logistical challenge in the port city of Toulouse, and as production ramped up, better options were needed. One was Boeing's use of Stratocruisers to carry very heavy loads, while another was conversion of four Boeing Spacelines, called "super guppies" – modified four-engine Boeing 377 Stratocruisers. However, notwithstanding industry jokes that "every Airbus gets delivered on

---

[31] The cost/safety trade-offs in high-reliability organizations are examined in a detailed study of the *Challenger* disaster. See Vaughn (1996). The O-ring theory is set in Kremer (1993). See also Deal (2004) and Dunbar and Garud (2009).

[32] The introduction of lean production and global logistics for supply chains, first seen in the auto sector, enhanced interest in modular design principles. For background, see Baldwin and Clark (2000).

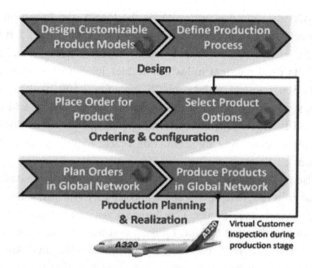

Figure 10 Airbus Production Planning System.
Source: Buergin et al. (2018).

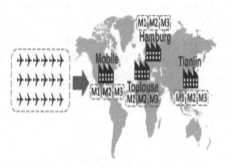

Figure 11 Aligning Customers Orders and Final Assembly.
Source: Buergin et al. (2018).

the wings of a Boeing," the super guppies were aging and had high operating costs. A new aircraft design was the only real option.

A dedicated Airbus team studied existing cargo models – Soviet designs like the Antonov An-124, the Antonov An-225, and the Ilyushin Il-76, Boeing models like the 747 and 767, Lockheed's C-5 Galaxy, and McDonnell Douglas's C-17 Globemaster III. In fact, Boeing actually offered to redesign the 767. In the end, Airbus decided to build a new cargo model, called the Beluga, with two Airbus partners, France's Aérospatiale and Germany's DASA, creating a 50–50 joint venture, and enlisted subcontractors for fifteen work plans, such as the fuselage, hydraulics, and the cargo loading systems. Construction began in September 1992, and the maiden flight took place two years later. Certification was approved by the EASA, the European Aviation Safety Agency, in October 1995, allowing the A300-600ST "Beluga" to enter service. The design offered flexibility to carry heavy loads (50 tons) on long flights (900 nautical miles), or lighter loads (40 tons) over longer distances (1,500 nautical miles), or 26 tons for 2,500 nautical miles. In short, Airbus was building its own ecosystem for its design and engineering team, and its dedicated, final assembly plants, starting in Toulouse but easily capable of extending its production reach, including to its American rival, the United States.

Airbus also followed Boeing's strategy of diversification beyond commercial jets to military aircraft, helicopters, space and security systems, and satellite and intelligence systems (see Figure 12). Airbus's senior management team had experience in coordinating technical design and manufacturing with multiple subcontracts from different countries, a geopolitical advantage, knowing that many countries and their governments preferred a policy to source locally. Product line diversification also allowed each firm to smooth out earnings in the very cyclical commercial airlines business, made worse by events like the 9-11 attack on the World Trade Center and COVID-19 pandemic, which brought the global airline sector to a standstill. In October 2020, Airbus created Aerostack, a joint venture with Elring Klinger, a component supplier with technology investments in fuel cell systems. Perhaps the ultimate irony was Boeing's willingness to join Airbus's bid for a £1 billion contract for the Royal Airforce, replacing its aging Puma helicopters.

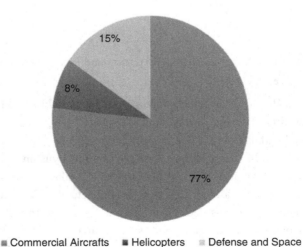

Figure 12 Airbus's total revenue diversification (2019).

Source: Airbus Financials, Forbes.

Boeing's Strategic Response to Airbus

As in war, so in economic rivalry there are many strategic options to address competitive threats. Some are defensive, like price cutting, seeking out new alliances, or appealing for government help. Some are proactive, like meeting competition directly, but providing better service, improved technology, or a better product. During the two decades with Airbus as Boeing's European rival, Boeing's Board of Directors and the senior management team were largely unphased. The operating assumption was straightforward: Airbus at best would garner market share with some European airlines, mostly legacy carriers owned by governments. Airbus's early success came, as expected, from sales and deliveries to leading airlines in Europe. But there was no secret about Airbus's wider ambitions.

Airbus's prolonged courtship of McDonnell Douglas for a merger as an entry platform to the US market failed, which was a massive relief in the Boeing C-suite but also a signal that more direct competition was simply postponed. Only slowly did Boeing appreciate the potential competitive dynamics if the Airbus–McDonnell Douglas merger had taken place, so Boeing decided to take preemptive action. Boeing's C-suite and board agreed to acquire McDonnell Douglas in 1996. In retrospect, it was a blessing in disguise for Airbus, but one not fully understood at this time. McDonald Douglas was a ruthless competitor in the cut-throat world of American defense procurement, with a winner-takes-all mentality to win contracts. Military contracts involve immense lobbying to members of Congress and defense firms, which locate factories in the home state of leading members who favor high defense spending. In reality, the game is more about winning the initial contract with cut-throat corporate practices, even if actual contract performance often comes above budget. (The F-35[33] is a typical, if unfair, case study – a fighter jet with a contract for $4 billion, starting at $35 million per aircraft, now above $80 m, and as high as $100 m with more additions over the life cycle of each plane.)

Boeing acquired McDonnell Douglas for $13.5 billion in a share swap, where each share of McDonnell Douglas was exchanged for 0.65 shares of Boeing. It

---

[33] The F-35 is designed and manufactured by Lockheed Martin with the initial plans for a one-size-fits-all solution as an aircraft for the US Airforce, Navy, and Marine Corps., and suitable for defense departments in other countries, including Japan, South Kora, and members of NATO. Overall lifetime costs were projected at $1.6 trillion, and planes per unit climbed to $80 million, up from $35 million per plane and remains the most expensive weapon systems ever built. However, the operating costs per plane are incredibly high – $36,000 per hour – the technical innovations added were more than necessary for its use in many missions, and spare parts and components are persistently late with many defects. In fact, service requirements for the Navy, Marines, and Air Force with proposed cost-savings proved illusory, with sharing only 20 percent of parts in common. For background, see Roblin (2021).

was the largest deal in aviation history, with $48 billion in sales and 200,000 employees. Boeing's Chairman, Philip Condit, confirmed that the merger talks started three years before but were finalized in December 1996, and then celebrated as two fierce rivals "creating a 'balanced and capable'" organization. The terms were actually negotiated by Condit and CEO of McDonnell Douglas, Harry C. Stonecipher, who became the largest individual shareholder, as well as the new President and CEO. In theory, these mergers are synergic, where combined firms would generate an estimated $6 billion in gross profits, and the liabilities such as combined debt would be only $5.5 billion, with $5.5 billion in ready cash. The reaction of aviation journalists and investment analysts was mixed. Did Boeing presume the merger would prevent firms from outside the US from acquiring McDonnell Douglas? Paine Webber analyst Jack Modzelewski provided some nationalist comfort, noting "it is great for America because it solidifies the commercial aircraft base in this country."[34]

In retrospect, was the merger a marriage of equals, or a reverse takeover of Boeing, as more McDonnell executives assumed senior positions at Boeing? Boeing had a history of a conservative C-suite approach, instilling an engineering model of innovative safety, reliability, and workplace collaboration culture, yet not unwilling to make bold decisions. The decision to break from the pack was shown by the launch of the 707, the wide-bodied 747, and the workhorse for low-cost airlines, the 737. On each occasion, Boeing's president consulted widely, especially with the leading airlines, but also with the technical team of engineers, knowing that any decision needed execution of a myriad of operational details.

The shift of headquarters to Chicago had broken the direct lines of communications and face-to-face meetings at Boeing. More tellingly, the Boeing C-suite quickly shifted the focus of executive time and attention away from technical engineering issues to the financial measures that appealed to Wall Street. The HQ relocation also broke a link between the home state that took pride in Boeing's achievements, and where President Roosevelt had once received a factory tour. New mantras became the order of the day – a top-down decision structure and governance based on plane deliveries, revenue growth, and share price. In reality, the Boeing C-suite took on a new financial engineering purpose, focusing on revenue growth and cost-cutting, with less expenditure on technical innovation and safety. This cultural shift was not immediately apparent at the levels of the board and C-suite. Gone were the leadership skills of Bill Allen, CEO from 1945 to 1968, demonstrated by what two McKinsey consultants called a capability "to pull people from several

---

[34] For background, see Vartabedian (1996).

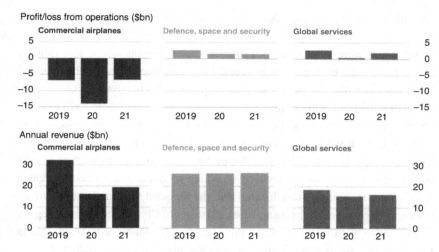

Figure 13 Breakdown of Boeing's main businesses.
Source: Boeing Financials.

layers down in the technical structure and put those individuals in charge of major projects, often with higher-salaried, more senior people reporting to them."[35] Headquarters and the C-suite set the corporate purpose and the mindset[36] of the senior managers and opened new fissures and a cultural gap between the technical and operational challenges, and Chicago headquarters' emphasis on Wall Street and shareholder values.

Boeing, with its diversified product portfolio (see Figure 13), made more complex by the merger of two product diversification firms in sectors as diverse as commercial airlines, defense, space, and security, mostly for the US military, allowed the C-suite and Boeing spokesmen to rationalize the headquarters move as a "new, leaner corporate center focused on shareholder value." One of the new executives was Harry Stonecipher, and his message was not lost on Boeing's workers and the union leadership – a message of corporate priorities: cashflow and profitability.[37] His reputation as an impatient, no-nonsense executive – first at General Electric's Aircraft Engine unit, then at McDonnell Douglas – reinforced

---

[35] See Peters and Waterman (1982), p. 311.

[36] In 1982, the two McKinsey consultants, Tom Peters and Robert Waterman, in their best-selling book, *In Search of Excellence*, singled out Boeing as a company to emulate, writing as follows: "[I]t appears to us that there is only one crucial concomitant to the excellent company's simple structural form: lean staff, especially at the corporate level. With the simple organizational form, fewer staff are required to make things tick."

[37] Investigative journalists saw Boeing's move to Chicago as one of a series of dubious moves and provided copious details of shifting corporate priorities. See, for example, reports by Gates (2019), Sell (2001), Useem (2019).

his outlook as a cost-cutting approach to production in Boeing's diverse product portfolio.

Resources were aligned on priorities like sales and marketing, and General Electric, now run by Jack Welch, became a model to emulate.[38] The financial benchmarks of Wall Street, like metrics of quarterly profits, return on net assets, and allocating free cashflow for share buybacks – 80 percent from 2013 to 2018, became C-suite priorities. By contrast, Airbus devoted more resources to increasing the R&D budget, now exceeding Boeing. The new CFO, Deborah Hopkins, recruited from General Motors Europe, was seen as a change agent whose new tasks at Boeing focused on which products and processes created value. The new headquarters, located near the financial district, was close to the Chicago Mercantile Exchange and the University of Chicago economics department, headed by Milton Friedman, and the Chicago Business School, advancing the ethos of capitalist profit-making and shareholder value. In fact, Boeing headquarters became a case study of financial engineering, and CEO, Phil Condit, rationalized the Chicago location decision as follows:

> Headquarters is supposed to be thinking longer-term: Where are markets going, have we positioned the company correctly, are we developing the right people, what's the compensation structure that we have? The kind of things that are not how-do-you-design-an-airplane stuff... How do you avoid getting deeply engaged in the day-to-day activity, and ignoring those strategic things?

Boeing's strategic shift coincided with the steady expansion of airline travel, and new airline startups, and new business models like Emirates Airlines or Virgin Air, flying nonstop city to city on long distance flights, for example, London to San Francisco, New York to Tokyo, or Dubai to Shanghai. It didn't take long for Airbus to match the plane lineup of Boeing 7-series – 787, 767, 757, 747, and 737 – based on number of seats, number of engines, and price range. Both Boeing and Airbus allowed the customer to choose the engine model from GE, Rolls-Royce, or Pratt & Whitney. Ironically, it was Airbus, not Boeing, who took the lead for plans of a superjumbo, with 550 seats and development costs of almost $12 billion, equal to 70 percent of the firm's annual revenue and a quarter of the combined sales revenue of Boeing and Airbus. It may not have been the "bet-the-firm" risk model, but it was close. Airbus's plan for the A-800-200 and an A380-900 model with 150-ton capacity for cargo was an audacious move, but Airbus appreciated that its four-nation ownership model

---

[38] General Electric's market cap went from $14 billion to $600 billion, and with priorities for any GE unit to be ranked globally as # 1 or 2. For background, with a nuanced view of Welch's tenure at GE, focusing on short termism, shareholder values, and unmanageable mergers, see Gelles (2022).

as a consortium had real advantages to create a risk culture.[39] Airbus's steady market growth, resources for R&D and new patents (Figure 14), plus greater acceptance of Airbus sales to US airlines confirmed the original corporate plans formulated in the early 1970s. In short, Airbus was on a roll.

Boeing's 747 and a "stretch" model might be close to Airbus's 550–600-seat design, but with far less start-up costs than Airbus. Estimates of $10 billion in development costs, not out of line with Airbus's projected development costs, which initially were an estimated $11.5 billion, became the topic in media reports. Subsidy support from the European Union's "launch aid" fund would lower the financial layout, as would support from leading subsuppliers and subcontractors, perhaps $3 billion. Boeing executives initiated a plan in January 1993 for a two-firm collaboration,[40] but industry insiders, and some American journalists, knew that Boeing's real interest was to delay or postpone a new rival model that would detract from the 747's steady cash flow (Figure 7), and would also preemptively thwart a new model planned by Mitsubishi Heavy Industries in Japan for a 150-seat aircraft model in 2007.

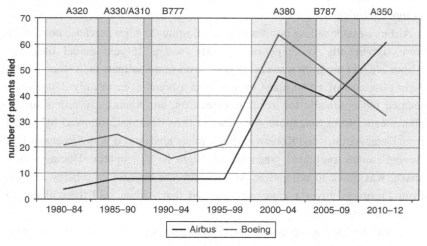

Figure 14 Patent trends at Airbus and Boeing 1985–2020.
Source: Beaugency et al. (2015).

---

[39] For a case study of the Super Jumbo rivalry, see Esty and Ghemawat (1982). The two authors quote a term "sporty bet" first used in John Newhouse's (1982) book on the commercial aircraft sector: "[W]hat really sets the commercial airplane business apart is the enormity of the risks, as well as the costs that must be accepted. They create an array of obstacles to profitability, hence viability, which discourages all but the bold and committed" (p. 3).

[40] For a game theory analysis of cooperative strategies or go-it-alone, or collaborate, see Fairchild and McGuire (2010).

Both firms knew that large, wide-bodied aircraft were technically feasible, as shown in military aircraft like the C-5. The real challenge was financial and technical, given the lead times from design to actual production, certification, and delivery. Given the complexity of such a large passenger plane, a new risk-uncertainty calculation was to ask suppliers to share the risk and commit financial backing. Boeing, aware of the Congressional cuts in US defense spending, had already followed this plan for its new 787, dubbed the Dreamliner, with a Japanese manufacturer, Mitsubishi Heavy Industry. They recruited other suppliers to join, including Kawasaki, a Japanese conglomerate with expertise in ship construction and simulators, to cite an example. Boeing's reaction to the Airbus plan for a superjumbo was a telling signal to the airline industry and to Boeing workers. The 747 had given Boeing a monopoly advantage, but the basic design was ageing fast, at a time when airlines like Qantas in Australia, ANA and Japan Airlines in Japan, and Emirates and Qatar Airways wanted planes for long-distance flights. Further, as many large airports like JFK in New York, Heathrow in London, and Charles de Gaulle in Paris faced more congestion, they also confronted political headwinds against constructing longer and more runways, as well as more terminal facilities.

Airbus's major selling point was basic: despite the high purchase cost, there were significantly lower operating costs over a 25-year model lifecycle. Airbus's R&D program was taking hold, with more patients than Boeing. The early estimates of 1,500 plane orders, with a break-even of only 250 planes, seemed too optimistic for aviation specialists, but when early orders for 75 planes came from Singapore Airlines and then Emirates, followed by orders from Qatar Airlines and Korean Airlines, many analysts on Wall Street saw that Boeing's once traditional preeminence might be in jeopardy. Boeing, taken aback, was quick to rationalize Airbus's success because of subsidy support from European governments, who assured that Airbus sold their planes to leading airlines in Europe.

In fact, Boeing wanted to push the US government to fight Airbus's subsidies to the World Trade Organization (WTO), the successor to the GATT, which led to a protracted seventeen-year trade dispute.[41] From a competitive stance, outside Europe, Airbus was building market share across the globe with its family of planes at different price points, and passenger/cargo space layout. Boeing has customarily downplayed its political role, but the firm was in fact immensely political, using its facilities to gain a plethora of tax breaks, subsidies, and even playing one US state against another. The American government's

---

[41] For background, see Kiestera (2012), Lombardi (2008), and Mathias (2005).

Table 1 Sales to China: Boeing vs. Airbus 2016–2021

Year	Boeing	Airbus
2021	7	124
2020	6	101
2019	45	178
2018	192	164
2017	161	181
2016	119	158

trade facility, the US Ex-Im Bank, which financed foreign airlines to purchase American products, was known worldwide as the Bank of Boeing.[42] It was standard practice at Boeing to gain political advantages, including challenge at the WTO to seek remedies from the EU subsidies for Airbus. This dispute[43] dates to an agreement signed in 2004, called the Agreement on Trade in Large Civil Aircraft (TLCA), which allowed a maximum 33 percent of development costs, government subsidies were prohibited, and indirect government (never really defined) was limited to a maximum of 3 percent of a firm's revenue or to a maximum of 4 percent of each company's turnover in civil aviation. In some circles, it was seen in Europe as an American strategy to apply "managed trade," with Japan the main target.

The US withdrew from the 2004 agreement and filed a new dispute with the WTO, claiming violations of the WTO agreement on Subsidies and Countervailing Measures (SCM), coincidently just as Airbus announced plans for two new models, the A-350 and the A-380. In many ways, the WTO dispute was a sideshow,[44] as Airbus steadily gained market share while Boeing was having internal production challenges (see Table 1). Airbus, in fact, had a strategy

---

[42] For historical background, see de Rugy (2020).

[43] In 2010, the WTO gave its verdict for the final panel report, and found that the British, German, and Spanish RLA was export contingent and therefore prohibited, but that the launch aid granted by the French government authorities did not violate WTO law. However, the WTO panel showed that certain infrastructure measures, corporate restructuring measures, and some research grants constituted specific subsidies for Airbus, but dismissed US claims loans provided by the European Investment Bank (EIB) as being specific subsidies (Kienstra, 2012). This bilateral conflict became inflamed by tariffs imposed by the Trump administration on allies like Europe and Canada on aluminum and steel "for security reasons." However, when President Joe Biden traveled to Europe in June 2021, the two governments of the US and EU settled the seventeen-year dispute over aircraft subsidies and suspended tariffs for five years. They also agreed to a bilateral working group to address nonmarket practices generally, including hidden government subsidies in places like China.

[44] The worry in US boardrooms was the competitive pressure of Japanese manufacturers, and political lobbying to seek government relief against Japanese competition; see McMillan (2022).

not unlike Toyota, with a three-part approach: build a strong customer base in the home market, have deep collaboration with subcontractors, and commit resources – time, effort, and money – to extend the product offerings across different price points using a platform design, with future marketing and production base in Boeing's own market. Boeing, like the Detroit car sector, was a late starter. In America, starting well before World War Two, models of production planning focused on small-batch production, assembly line production of large batches, and process systems.[45] Two decades later, after Toyota applied its famed *kaizen* principles of constant improvement, consulting firms and a few academics extolled the benefits of lean production. Boardrooms in America were less informed, including auto manufacturers in Detroit, or Boeing in Seattle.[46] By this time, Toyota even had its own consulting firm to assure best practices were followed across its global network of factories (Dyer and Nobeoka, 2000).

Bruce Henderson, the former head of Boston Consulting group, eloquently described the system: "Just-in-time is a colloquial expression for describing a philosophy and technique that may be the ace in the game of manufacturing productivity. In the history of the Industrial Revolution, it may rank with interchangeable parts, precision gauge blocks, assembly lines, time and motion studies, and powered conveyors" (McMillan, 1996, p. 283). In their study of the global automobile sector, three economists from MIT published a study, *The Machine That Changed the World*, referring not to Toyota but its production system (Womack et al., 1990).[47]

---

[45] Some of this theoretical research on production systems came from the American war effort, when the United States excelled at the mobilization of economists for the Departments of Treasury, Agriculture, and Commerce, and the Office of Price Administration, in topics such as search (antisubmarine warfare), resource allocation (raw materials supplies and use for tanks or ships), computation (e.g. code-breaking), weather and bombing (altitudes, day vs. night), and time series estimations (e.g. casualties), with work originating at the Cowles Commission. New research disciplines were developed in operations research, based on mathematical studies comprising highway traffic, railway transportation, ocean shipping, inventory management, crop rotation, and activity analysis. In the post-war period, a leading center for these developments was Carnegie Institute of Technology, now Carnegie Mellon University, and the business school, the Graduate School of Industrial Administration, with eight Nobel laureates. For background, see McMillan (2017) and Schwab and Starbuck (2016).

[46] Useem (2019) describes the production at Boeing as follows: "[T]he assembly lines of América's leading exporter were morasses of inefficiency. Airplanes were built more like customized houses, with airlines able to select from 109 shades of white paint, 20,000 gallery and lavatory arrangements, and even contained prayer rooms with devices that pointed to Mecca ('Mecca meters'). Overseeing it all was an appalling system known as 'effectivity' which dates from Boeing's World War II bomber days and used a manual numbering system to keep track of an airplane's four million parts and 170 miles of wiring; changing a part of a 737's landing gear thus meant remembering 464 pages of drawings. Yes, there had been attempts at automation, but by the early '90s they had metastasized into 450 computer systems, few of which could talk to one another."

[47] Today the literature on Toyota and lean production is enormous, and often singles out applications to different functions like logistics and supply management, human resources, supplier–subcontract relations, for example, and often has applications to different industrial sectors, such

Despite the time lag, Boeing finally took action. In the early 1980s, senior managers at Boeing invited JIT gurus like W. Edward Deming and J. M. Jurin to visit Seattle to address managers and workers. Statistical process control (SPC) was adopted later that decade. Boeing decided to benchmark production processes with General Electric, and adopted techniques learned from DeltaPoint, a JIT consulting firm. Its first test case was Boeing's Arnprior fabrication plant located near Ottawa. The first serious approach to learn JIT came only in 1990, just when the US government cancelled cost-plus contracts in the defense sector. Senior Boeing executives, board members, and supervisors visited Japan, to learn from companies, industry associations, and consulting firms well versed on Toyota's JIT approach.

Over two weeks, the Boeing entourage studied eight Japanese companies, ranging from Sony, Toyota, Hitachi, and Mitsubishi Heavy Industries, with an aim to focus on the five S's: Sort, Simplify, Sweep, Standardize, and Self-Discipline. Every area was required to progress from level 1 through 5 of 5S. Massive amounts of material were put in surplus, recycled, or simply discarded. Boeing conducted more seminars, trials, and trips to Japan – including a visit to study Toyota's production system – in an effort to improve work processes, otherwise known at Boeing as AIW, Accelerated Improvement Workshops. In retrospect, Boeing's efforts, while laudable, were piecemeal, often delegated to particular executives, or confined to areas like the Fabrication Division. Unlike Toyota, Boeing never adopted a systems-wide approach, despite establishing a Lean Manufacturing Office, which only exposed piecemeal, fragmented efforts. By contrast, from the beginning, Airbus applied lean production

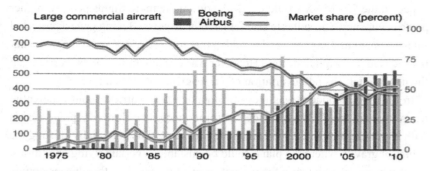

Figure 15 Airbus and Boeing: deliveries and market share 1975–2010.

---

as retailing, healthcare, and not-for-profit. For background of the tools, mechanisms, and processes, see Abegglen and Stalk (1985), Dyer and Nobeoka (2010), McMillan (1985, 2006), Shingo (1989), and Takeuchi et al. (2008).

principles over all operations, including in the factories of the subassembly plants located across Europe, and its two assembly plants in America.

Inadequate pilot training and insufficient pilot experience are problems worldwide, but they do not excuse the fatally flawed design of the Maneuvering Characteristics Augmentation System (MCAS) that was a death trap. – Captain Chesley "Sully" Sullenberger

5 The Boeing 737 MAX Debacle

By most measures – clever design, planes sold and in service, and overall profitability – the 737 was a star in Boeing's portfolio of aircraft models. The 737-100 started service in 1969 with the first customer, Lufthansa Airlines. Over four decades, Boeing made regular improvements, including the lengthened model, the 737-300, and airlines around the world knew the 737 series – 737-100 to 737-800. Pilots and cabin crews loved the 737 narrow-body, twin-jet plane, and airlines were devoted customers for its flexibility, easy maintenance, and relatively low cost per seat/mile. By 2010, the 737 was a forty-year design. Just when the Boeing C-suite had plans to introduce a totally new model, there was an unforeseen announcement in December 2010 that Airbus was developing a new family of planes, the A320, and the media wanted a strategic response.

Four months later, in March 2011, Boeing announced the 737 MAX, a next-generation plane expected to be ready by 2017, a six-year development time. Airlines welcomed the news of the 737 MAX, with its longer-range, quieter engines, and better fuel efficiency, thus lower operating and maintenance costs. Leading low-cost airlines like Southwest in America, and Ryan Air in Europe expected the 737 MAX would be ideal, combining more flights per day, higher plane occupancy, and suitable size for smaller airports. Boeing gave a projected sales estimate of 4,000 planes but added that the 737 MAX was one of regular upgrades to the original design. However, various aviation experts worried that the new model was not a variation of the original 737 plus modifications.

In fact, their concern was more profound. They worried about a potential design flaw in the 737 MAX. Boeing's pronouncement showed a plane design with larger engines and placement moved forward, thus potentially shifting the center of gravity where the plane could be unstable in certain flying conditions. More worrisome still was a feature not fully appreciated by the airlines hoping to acquire the MAX, or by the US government certification body, the Federal Aviation Administration (FAA). Clearly, Boeing wanted to assure commonality with previous versions of the 737, where the mechanical design would receive FAA certification to meet demand forecasts. However, any modifications in the 737 MAX other than new engines and more advanced avionics would lengthen the FAA certification process, beyond the deliveries in 2017. Obviously, existing customers wanting to acquire this new 737 MAX could use their existing crews and pilots, without incurring more time and investments for additional training, a regulatory necessity when a new model needs certification. In fact, any delay for retraining would slow down the certification process and thereby add time – a precious resource in a time-based production schedule – for final approval. The impact on Boeing's cash flow could be immense.

Boeing proceeded on its schedule. But two fatal crashes, the first on October 29, 2018, at Jakarta, Indonesia, thirteen minutes after takeoff, killing 189 passengers and crew, and the second in Ethiopia in March 2019, claiming another 156 lives, received global media coverage – on TV, social media, and newspapers. For a company like Boeing, where the media expected senior management to have expertise in crisis management, the firm set new standards for mismanagement. Media coverage gave aviation experts – including executives who had experience working at Boeing – nonstop coverage. Investigative journalists at the *New York Times* and other outlets like *The Seattle Times* and Bloomberg began drilling down on the likely cause, spoke with one voice, and ruled out a missile attack, a pilot suicide mission, or other causes, including the weather, pilot error, or faulty controls from older models.

In fact, in both flight crashes, the planes were flying in good weather, the pilots and crew were experienced with the 737, and there were no signs of fuel shortages, engine failure, or faulty equipment like landing gear. Indeed, both airlines had a good record for safety. Many aviation experts with knowledge of the FAA certification processes focused on a technical innovation introduced for the 737 MAX, a software package for anti-stall that controls the angle of the plane in the unlikely event of an engine stall. Called a Maneuvering Characteristics Augmentation System (MCAS), this software was designed to provide compensation for the new powerful engines and their forward placement. However, Boeing hadn't disclosed the existence of this software to the pilots and crews until after the first plane fatality. Nor were there any suggestions, let alone requirements, that the pilots should take simulation training to know and understand how the MCAS software actually worked.

Within hours of both crashes, Boeing had issued almost identical statements of condolence to the victims' relatives, and the cooperation with the public investigators. But media-savvy Boeing executives knew that these pablum statements would not satisfy the major airlines, governments, and their transportation and aviation specialists, let alone the flying public. Boeing issued another statement, adding an Operations Manuel Bulletin (OMB), directed at pilots and airline administrators to understand the special circumstances of erroneous data inputs. However, Indonesia's National Transport Safety Board issued its own commentary, much more pointed and even accusatory, stating that Boeing's flight manual for the 737 MAX was "incomplete."

In America, by law, the FAA must approve and certify each model. Globally, FAA's good housekeeping seal of approval was seen as a model of certification, working at relatively low cost with an outstanding record of safety, thus accepted by governments in Europe, Canada, Japan, and most other countries. One consequence of the Boeing MAX debacle is the breakdown of Boeing's traditional and close cooperation with the FAA, and this growing rupture had many direct and indirect results. In fact, a major concern became an open sore, namely the extra time needed to check each part, component, and subsystem for safety. It also required extra time to design and manufacture new parts, an increase in time and cost for international certification, and the need to assure pilots domestically and internationally.[48]

The 737 MAX debacle put both Boeing and the FAA, and their differing versions of events, into the media spotlight. Some Boeing senior executives wanted to quicken the pace of certification, as some insiders knew the real financial debt burdens were climbing, leaving aside potential lawsuits from leading customers like Southwest and the relatives of the crash victims. More tellingly, Boeing's board had approved a protracted series of annual share buy-backs, costing about $43 billion, so Boeing didn't have a cash nest egg to draw on. Facing unparalleled scrutiny, the FAA wanted a clear and transparent plan that the software system was indeed redesigned and fixed before certification was granted. Some Boeing engineers even floated the idea that FAA should certify the plane on its own, without cooperation and collaboration from regulators in Europe, Canada, or Japan, reflecting a misunderstanding of the problem at hand, and a pernicious culture where Boeing executives were aligned with Wall Street, quarterly earnings, and the bottom line. In response, the FAA quietly issued its own statement that such an approach would be "untenable."

Investigative reporters, including the highly respected Bloomberg journalist, Peter Robinson, exposed this deteriorating relationship[49] between Boeing and the FAA, once seen as cooperative and sharing, but now seen as testy and adversarial. In fact, Stephen Dickson, the head of the FAA, publicly berated

---

[48] For Boeing, the 737 MAX was not an isolated example of faulty design, on-going quality problems, and plane certification. The outspoken comments of Sir Tim Clark, CEO of Emirates Airlines (Spaeth, 2021), typified both the public statements and private thoughts of Boeing's major airline customers: " . . . but when we know the normal rules were compromised in the MAX program, and this aircraft was built at the same time under the same regime. I can't understand why the 777X with all its novelties was ticketed as a derivative, while it's not when you build a new aircraft. The MAX was a derivative of the 737NG, but was it? The issue of the 777-9X at the moment is one of certification. We need clarification that it has been built according to the rules we will accept."

[49] See Robinson (2019).

Boeing CEO Dennis Mullenberg, who insisted on a speedy approval process. He had briefed President Donald Trump, who faced a fall election in 2020 and timeline estimates for the plane's return to service. Both knew that disruptions and canceled flights would lead to angry responses from the public and from Boeing customers.

Both Boeing and the FAA also knew that anger was building from various stakeholders – wary legislators in Congress, irate relatives of the victims (who disapproved Boeing executives attending the funerals), public criticism by pilot unions, and open criticism of the CEOs of some airlines, like Emirates. In 2019, clearly an *annus horribilis* for Boeing, transport regulators from Brazil, Canada, and Europe flew to Seattle to get a full update. Expecting a thorough examination on the 737 MAX and the underlying reasons for the two crashes, they witnessed Boeing executives showing only an anodyne presentation, greatly annoying the attendees. One FAA executive admitted with a vast understatement on Boeing's presentation, "We were looking for a lot more rigour . . . they were not ready."

The following month, Boeing's CEO, Dennis Muilenburg, an introverted engineer, attended the annual gathering in Wyoming of the secretive organization, the Conquistadores del Cielo. This meeting of leading airline CEOs was informal and casual, and offered a chance to hear Boeing's version of the MAX debacle, and the steps underway, and even settle quietly and diplomatically the real void among airlines which depended on Boeing's delivery of 737s. To everyone's surprise, Muilenburg avoided most of the sessions, took long bike rides alone, and avoided most of the happy hour drinking sessions before socializing over meals. Even in the Boeing C-suite, growing impatience and unhappiness were evident.

Two months later, in October, the Boeing board removed his title as Chairman, a serious indictment to insiders but seen in the industry as an innocuous governance play. Just before his appearance at Congressional hearings, Muilenburg faced withering criticism of the firm's behavior (and unrelenting complaints from victims' relatives). He disclosed a series of emails dating from 2016, where a Boeing pilot openly complained that the MCAS system could act unpredictably in a flight simulator, which was an open admission the pilot "basically lied to the regulators (unknowingly)." By this time, Boeing had infuriated key stakeholders, illustrated by a release of a single paragraph letter from FAA CEO, Stephen Dickson, for an explanation of "Boeing's delay in disclosing the document to the safety regulator." In the end, Boeing shut down the 737 MAX assembly line in December 2019. On Wall Street, Boeing's stock price fell by 22 percent, and leading subcontractors stopped their own production runs. Over 8,000 sub-suppliers were left in a lurch. Ten months after the second crash, Boeing had no clear plan to fix the software system.

The final 250-page report of the Indonesia investigation appeared in October 2019, which placed some of the blame on the pilots and crew but noted that data from the recovered flight recorder showed that the MCAS software forces the nose of the plane to move downward twenty-six times in only ten minutes. In reality, the report noted, "Boeing failed in its design and development of the Max, and the FAA failed in its oversight of Boeing and its certification of the aircraft," and cited a litany of design failures, which led to shortcuts: "[The crashes] were the horrific culmination of a series of faulty technical assumptions by Boeing's engineers, a lack of transparency on the part of Boeing's management, and grossly insufficient oversight by the FAA." By this time, Boeing had already issued a bulletin to pilots for procedures with flight control issues, and the FAA issued similar warnings with an Emergency Airworthiness Directive. It was the first time that airline pilots learned about the existence of the MCAS software on the 737 MAX.

The blame game was shifting. It took a more combustible form when the pilots union openly challenged the veracity of the instruction and equipment and the 737 MAX plane itself. More intensive probing of Boeing's internal processes exposed two issues that illustrated the brutal effects of a cost-cutting approach. Union spokesmen for Boeing engineers confirmed that tight budgets to prevent cost overruns left a quality and inspection vacuum, and if workers found trouble spots in the production process, they were labeled as *troublemakers*. Other spokesmen complained that management rejected recommendations for a safety add-on with implications for potential (pilot) training impact. One Boeing engineer, Curtis Ewbank, filed an internal ethics report that Boeing management had squelched the errors in the AOA sensors, and his later remarks, widely quoted in the press, left no doubt who was to blame: "I was willing to stand up for safety and quality ... Boeing management was more concerned with cost and schedule than safety or quality."[50]

By this time, Boeing's operations and history faced withering scrutiny. Boeing's relocation of the C-suite to Chicago and the new culture obsessed with financial engineering tools, away from an emphasis on safety and reliability, became a case study of reputation damage. As one media report published in *The Atlantic* noted,[51] "new management even went so far as 'maligning and marginalizing engineers as a class.'" A BBC program, *Panorama,* broadcast a documentary in July 2019 called *Boeing's Killer Planes*, which quoted Adam Dickson, a former Boeing engineer, who reinforced the internal priorities of the C-suite: "[T]here was a lot of interest and pressure on the certification and

---

[50] For background, see Kitroeff and Gilles (2019).   [51] See Useem (2019).

analysis engineers in particular, to look at any changes to the Max as minor changes."

In June 2019, Bloomberg's Peter Robison (2019) disclosed that Boeing had subcontracted development and testing of software, employing temporary workers at $9 an hour, mainly to two Indian firms. In response, Boeing claimed the firm did not rely on engineers from either HCL or Cyient for the MCAS software. Many other multinationals, including GE and US defense contractors, replicated Boeing sales efforts in India and brought big dividends like a $2.2 billion deal for SpiceJet Ltd and an order for 100 B-737 Max 8 for Air India. However, the reaction from the flying public was immediate and damaging, and aviation experts openly challenged Boeing's decision-making, given how the design flaw meant pilots could not override the software control system when sensors provided false input data to the computer system. NBC quoted a very unhappy US Senator Richard Blumenthal: "The fact is the FAA decided to do safety on the cheap which is neither cheap nor safe and put the fox in charge of the hen house."

During the early months of 2020, America's FAA continued to support Boeing's version of events, as did some US airlines, as well as President Donald Trump. Boeing attempted in public to be openly transparent, while many Boeing executives felt this iconic firm had lost its sure-footed manufacturing prowess and openly displayed hubris without remorse. It was a signal of hubris and myopic countenance when Boeing executives also inflamed the passions of key customers like Southwest and Ryanair; plus members of Congress and the chairman of the House Transportation Committee, Peter de Fazio from Oregon; as well as the pilots union. The public at large, now tired of anodyne public apologies, received no real assurances that the software problems were being addressed. A few American senators called for a grounding of all 737 MAX planes "as a temporary measure," but with huge implications, financial and managerial, for Boeing and, by extension, the audit systems used by the FAA for certification.

Clearly, Boeing hoped to buy time, knowing the decline in production meant cash outlays were climbing fast. In fact, Boeing's internal forecasts showed that estimates were on track to complete fifty-seven planes a month but reduce production to fifty-two and then only forty-two planes, which had real financial consequences on cashflow outlays. As news spread through the industry in America, China and the European Union suspended all flight operations of the 737 MAX, quickly followed by Canada and Japan. Soon after, the FAA finally grounded the 737 MAX. Indonesia's top regulatory body officially referred to the Boeing–FAA relationship as "the Americans," and many experts called the FAA a case study of regulatory capture.

Boeing share prices dropped 2 percent, key subcontractors stopped production, and their 8,000 subcontractors began to lay off workers (Waldmeir, 2019). Large Boeing customers like Ryan Air, expecting delivery of seventy-five planes, received only eleven. Boeing's first-mover advantage for this flexible, narrow-bodied aircraft was changing the competitive dynamics, diminishing Boeing's pricing power, because Airbus could offer equivalent or better deals. Ryan Air was publicly asking Airbus to discount prices during their negotiations for a large contract with Boeing, allegedly getting their order with huge discounts to the asking price.[52] For Boeing, the real cost of the 737 MAX meant rising outlays for factory maintenance and abnormal expenditures to fix the design flaw. To add to Boeing's growing internal problems, a crash of a China Eastern Airlines flight in China in March 2022, killing 123 passengers and a crew of nine, was a Boeing 737-800. This tragedy, totally unrelated to the mechanical and software dysfunctions of the 737 MAX, further damaged Boeing's reputation in China. Boeing's shareholder ethos lay in ruins.

> [T]his mad scramble for cash and the existential urge to "preserve cash in challenging periods" comes after this master of financial engineering – instead of aircraft engineering – blew, wasted, and incinerated $43.4 billion on buying back its own shares, from 2013 until the financial consequences of the two 737 Max crashes finally forced the company to end the practice. That $43.3 billion would come in really handy right now. – Wolf Richter in Wolf Street Report

6 Boeing Stalls and Then Declines

Most organizations, large and small, face the potential of a stall position, when a company's growth rate slips into what can be a prolonged decline (Olsen and Van Bevin, 2008). This position describes Boeing today, based on such performance benchmarks as market share, R&D, market capitalization, order book, and commercial customers. Even in financial returns, Boeing's five-year record is negative 20 percent compared to Airbus's 31.84 percent gain; its ten-year return, 158.90 gain, compares to Airbus's 246.04 return. In a Schumpeterian framework of creative destruction, firms big and small face new rivals, new product lines, and new technologies. Technological disruption can also face the innovative leader (Christensen, 2012), where competitive

---

[52] See Ryan Air's order with Boeing. It is well known in the airline industry that OEM list prices for different models rarely conform to the negotiated price, even more so with large orders.

rivalry allows product substitutes, often at the low end, but also in underserved sectors, or exploiting new bundles of technology, as shown in the smartphone sector against the desktop computer.

The study of organizational failure[53] puts far less emphasis on economic issues, such as financial and revenue shortfalls, or even technology threats. Boeing's move to Chicago was a misreading of governance responsibility that top executives understood the technical features of aircraft design and manufacturing, and the growing risk that such tightly coupled linkages can lead to design failures. Modern jet aircraft manufacturing is an example of high-reliability organizations, requiring new forms of accountability, and social interaction, where defects and perturbations are transmitted rapidly with no compromises for defects and errors.

Often the first move for a company in trouble is to replace the CEO, a path followed by Boeing with the appointment of David Calhoun. He had a diverse background, working at McKinsey, then as head of GE's unit for aircraft engines and avionics. He became an avid reader of a series of media and investment reports that Boeing was following the path of GE's decline, from $120 per share to less than $5.00 at one point. What, in fact, were the real strategic options facing Boeing's C-suite? Was one scenario a breakup of Boeing by unrelated product lines, following the new path eventually enacted at General Electric? Or was a better and more appropriate metaphor the case of General Motors, which once commanded a 70 percent market share in North America, before facing bankruptcy in 2009.

As noted, decreased financial performance is often a symptom of underlying organizational dysfunctions, like high executive turnover and flawed quality control practices. Boeing's narrative to the public was to focus on Airbus's special advantages, such as EU subsidies and bribes to third-world airlines. However, like GM, Boeing has been steadily losing market share in its own market, and like Toyota, Airbus has gained a technology edge with its production system, and investments in Canada and the United States. Airbus borrowed heavily from the ideas and principles of lean production. Boeing, in fact, had to develop similar systems, but only for one model, the 787 (Figure 16).

---

[53] The literature on organizational decline and failure, akin to pathology studies in the medical world, is based on pathologies of executive myopia, faulty feedback mechanisms, and accepted routines that thwart capacities for learning, sense-making, and adaption and has an interdisciplinary focus. See Amburgey et al. (1993), Baumard and Starbuck (2005), Cannon and Edmondson (2005), Ciborra et al. (2000), Garicano and Rao (2016), Lorange and Nelson (1987), McMillan and Overall (2017), Perrow (1984), Sheppard and Chowdhury (2005), and Snook (2000) for representative organizational perspectives.

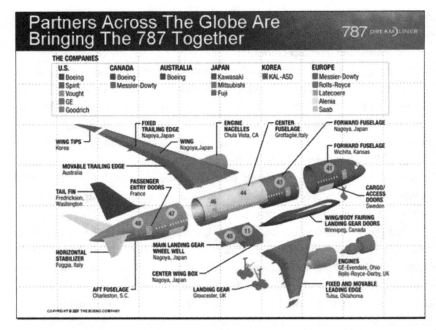

Figure 16 The globally based manufacture and assembly of the Boeing
Dreamliner.

Source: Boeing Corporation.

Airbus had another competitive strength, a network advantage, which combines internal design and production capabilities with external collaboration with firms, sectors, and countries that support and reinforce shared learning and innovation. Boeing's financial plight was well known beyond the commercial plane sector, thanks to extensive media coverage, and aviation experts well understood the firm's cultural DNA as a financial engineering company.[54] Investigative journalists exposed the changes, where Boeing lost its reputation as an advanced engineering powerhouse, managing a financial portfolio of aerospace products with so-so financial results, even on models introduced years before, like the 747, the 737, or the 787.[55]

Boeing was experiencing the ubiquitous vocabulary of shareholder governance, where shareholder value was the mantra for investors (Rappaport, 1998) and Boeing's new value proposition. For the US public, now fully aware of Boeing's internal dysfunctions with the 737 MAX debacle, it became especially

---

[54] For background, see Muellerleile (2009) and McGuire (2007).

[55] See, for example, numerous articles and books by Useem (2019) and Robison (2021) documenting these organizational dysfunctions, but the same view was widespread among key investment bank analysts on Wall Street.

hard to rationalize the huge costs overrun for Airforce One, an upgraded 747 replacing the aged model launched in 1980. The new Air Force One was subject to more scrutiny when President Donald Trump, complaining about cost overruns, called for design changes. This contract, originally worth $3.9 billion, climbed to $4.3 billion, with expected completion extended to 2026. Even worse, this contract had terms negotiated as a fixed price deal, where cost overruns were covered by Boeing, but this contract was not an isolated case. Boeing's CEO, Dennis Muilenburg, negotiated other deals such as the widely publicized KC-46A fuel tanker, the T-7A Red Hawk pilot trainer, the MQ-25 drone, and the Starliner space capsule. Consider the following examples.

➢ Growing losses of the $1.32 billion contract for KC-46 tankers for the US Air Force, mainly from production inefficiencies.
➢ New defects in Boeing's older models of the 737.
➢ Delays and higher costs of $6.5 billion for the 777X program, and fears of reduced demand for a twin aisle with four jet engines.
➢ Abnormally higher costs of $550 million for reengineering fixes for Boeing's Remote Vision System.
➢ Continued losses on its satellite product line, over $300 m a quarter.
➢ Continuing production problems with the 787, temporarily grounded in 2011 after its maiden flight, but increased inspection showed design flaws that slowed delivery.
➢ Boeing faced a lawsuit for theft of intellectual property from a Colorado-based firm in a case, Wilson Aerospace LLC v. Boeing Co, U.S. District Court, No. 23-00847, including using Wilson's trade secrets without getting full instructions to build and install without creating safety risks.

As noted, David Calhoun became CEO in October 2019 in a bloodless coup, allowing Muilenburg to exit with a remuneration package worth an estimated $60 million. In 2019, just before the shareholders' annual meeting, two proxy advisory firms, Institutional Shareholder Services Inc. (ISS), and Glass, Lewis & Co., called for governance changes at Boeing, including separation of the CEO and Board Chairman, and removal of the head of the Audit Committee who was also in charge of risk management, including aviation safety. The board rejected this change, and so did the shareholder vote at the annual meeting. Six months later, the board finally relented and chose a new chairman, David Calhourn, who spoke to the media about the board's confidence in the CEO, Dennis Muilenburg: "From the vantage point of our Board, Dennis has done everything right" (Driskill, 2019; Kitroeff and Gelles, 2019).

His time on Boeing's board taught him something about how big companies stall, and as the coauthor of a management book, *How Companies Win*, knew his "To Do" agenda kept getting longer. Rebranding and advertising slogans are a hapless exercise for firms like Boeing, which is not in the consumer goods sector.[56] Boeing's share price follows hand in hand with actual financial performance, and delayed plane deliveries (Figure 17), as continuing corporate losses (a $10.5 profit in 2018, losses of $11.9 in 2020, and $4.2 million in 2021) go beyond the 737 MAX disaster. From a high stock price of over $440 in March 2019, Boeing shares had fallen steadily to a low of $91 and a market cap of only $70 billion as market watchers at home and around the world saw declining deliveries in 2020, 80 percent less than in 2018, and only a third of Airbus's (see Figure 18). Clearly, as a duopoly sector, Boeing's survival is not in doubt, because no one in Washington would allow it to go under due to a foreign takeover, bankruptcy, national security reasons, or job losses.

Nonetheless, Boeing shows few signs that it really understands its corporate rival, Airbus, and is still only too willing to blame the EU's launch of subsidies to rationalize Airbus's delivery success (Figure 18) and its global acceptance among leading airlines, including US carriers like Delta, which signed a deal in 2023 for 100 planes to expand its fleet.

Boeing's financial distress coincided with slowed delivery dates, and models still needing certification approvals put a squeeze on cash flow, just when cash liquidity is required to meet expected backorder demand. Further, Boeing's

Airbus built more planes and won more orders than Boeing thanks to its dominance in the single-aisle market, where the A320neo goes up against the 737 MAX. Boeing fared better in sales of the more expensive widebody jets because Airbus lost large orders canceled by AirAsiaX and Qatar Airways.

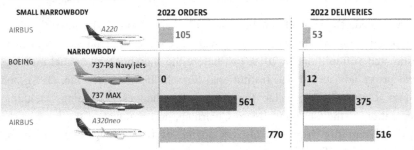

Figure 17 In 2022 jet orders and deliveries, Airbus maintained its advantage over Boeing.

Source: The Seattle Times (January 10, 2023).

---

[56] For this flawed approach, see Welch (2021).

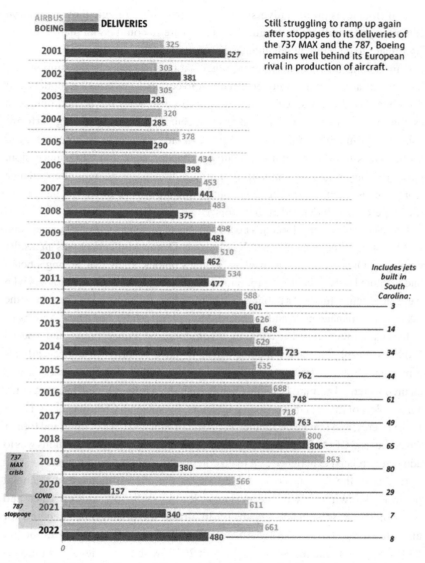

Figure 18 Airbus is the world's no. 1 jetmaker for the fourth successive year.
Source: The Seattle Times (April 10, 2024).

diversification beyond commercial aircraft in defense, space, and national security, with an estimated growth in the multibillion-dollar sector, is the stated rationale to relocate to Arlington, Virginia. However, American incumbent rivals, including Lockheed Martin, Northrup Grumman, General Dynamics, and Raytheon Technologies, are equal or bigger in size and show much higher investment returns than Boeing, both in the short run and the long run. In the case of Boeing, is product diversification a signal of a strategic flaw, a situation caught in the middle with declining market share in commercial planes, but no significant technological advantages in other sectors?

Can Boeing bring about internal organizational reforms in decision styles, incentives, and improved governance? Conventional governance models call for a board of directors, with two people holding separate but related functions as chairman and CEO, with the latter overseeing the firm's operating performance and profitability for each product segment, plus separate committees to probe issues for annual audits, executive compensation, and CEO succession, based on four pillars: accountability, fairness, transparency, and independence from management. (The criteria set out by the New York Stock Exchange call for 75 percent as independent directors.)

For historical reasons, Boeing's board consists of members who are independent. In 2019, at the time of the 737 MAX crisis, only Dennis Muilenburg was an insider employee. Outside groups, as well as Boeing's unions, knew that Boeing's board had instituted a share buyback program, strengthening links with shareholders who were large equity funds. As public pressure mounted, and more angst arose from the FAA, senior management, and the board, Muilenburg established a new Aerospace Safety Committee. Another addition, a committee on Public Policy and Special Projects, meant that board members had to have security clearance and had a mandate to ensure safety by reviewing existing policies and processes. It was chaired by retired admiral Edmund Giambastiani Jr., a former Vice-Chairman of the Joint Chiefs of Staff, and two Boeing directors, Lynn Good, Chairman and CEO of Duke Energy, and Lawrence Kellner, President of Emerald Creek Group and former Chairman and CEO of Continental Airlines. One of its first recommendations was to add safety-related experience as a main criterion to appoint new directors.

By 2020, the Boeing board had to assess the overall damage to financial position, knowing that in the previous decade, with low interest rates and inflation, there was steady expansion in airline travel and more demand for aircraft. Before the two 737 MAX accidents, Boeing's share price climbed to $441, revenues reached $101.1 billion in 2018, with record levels of deliveries, 806, and 893 net orders, and operating margins had steadily improved, from 8.2 percent in 2014 to 11.9 percent. The board raised the quarterly dividend in December 2018 by 20 percent and launched a new share repurchase program of $20 billion (Figure 19). By contrast, the new decade saw rising interest rates, more geopolitical tension, energy shortages, and threats from climate change, and Boeing and its senior management team still faced a range of intractable challenges, including certification of the Boeing MAX, the 787, and the updated 777.

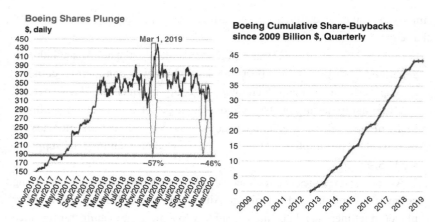

Figure 19 Boeing's financial engineering dilemma.

Source: Adapted from Wolf Richter, Boeing Crashes (Mar 11, 2020).

Boeing's governance under Calhoun as CEO and the board decided to follow a "stay the course" strategy, with the hope that internal hiring and a new technological research center near the third location for headquarters in Arlington, Virginia, would return the company to its former glory. That approach meant regular upgrades to its dated models – the 737, the 787, and the 777, providing revenues from a growing order book to pay down its debt. Recent efforts show that Boeing is now cashflow positive, but that is hardly the outcome of a once pioneering aircraft manufacturer. Boeing still trails Airbus in annual investments in R&D, with its plans to challenge traditional designs, such as supersonic planes with very high speeds, like the SST model planned four decades ago. Boeing's financial dilemma is to stay cash flow positive, and hope that a growing order book will remove the existential threat of insolvency, especially in the case of another serious plane fatality of the 737 MAX. Clearly, there can be no concrete plans to invest in new designs (even though new startups like Boom are collaborating with some airlines on a new sonic aircraft) or in new, smaller planes used as taxis, as well as autonomous pilot aircraft, backed by Airbus.

Emphasis on corporate scale, market power, sheltered support from governments to provide tax advantages, and the nationalist card can influence corporate decision making, and Boeing is prepared to play that card in the face of hardball competition from Airbus and potential rivals like China's aerospace sector. Both defense firms and manufacturers like Boeing and Airbus also focus on the space sector, often in the past with NASA taking a leadership role (Brunberg, 1990). More Boeing board members have a background in the US military, so an incrementalistic strategy may seem warranted, even if major airline customers and Boeing employees take a different view. An article in Forbes[57] outlined the challenges:

> In 2019, the last normal year before the pandemic, the aerospace industry generated $148 billion in exports, 85% of which was commercial content. Aerospace is the last major technology category in which the U.S. generates a substantial trade surplus. But without Boeing, that isn't likely to continue. Many of the small and medium-size domestic companies in the sector survive because they are suppliers to Boeing (80% of Boeing's commercial suppliers are U.S.-based).
>
> Although companies like Raytheon can keep making good returns by selling commercial engines and avionics to Airbus, the loss of Boeing as a first-tier player in jetliners would be the worst blow to American manufacturing since the auto industry skirted bankruptcy during the subprime crisis 14 years ago. Some analysts might argue that at this point Boeing should sell its defense unit and focus on the core commercial business, since that's where most of the revenue and backlog resides. However, that would weaken the enterprise over the long run, because demand for jetliners is cyclical and the company needs income from non-commercial sources to sustain itself in lean years.

7 Discussion and Conclusion

The history of Boeing and its founder illustrates the entrepreneurial will of many people who saw the potential of aircraft not only as a means to travel long distances, but in terms of the thrill of conquering Mother Nature, with heavier leads, higher speeds, and direction. As the commercial airline sector enters the third decade of the twenty-first century, the duopoly among two firms – the market leader, Airbus Industries, known as EADS, the European Aeronautic Defense and Space Company; and Boeing, a diversified American firm with headquarters in Arlington, Virginia. Today, Airbus's growing market share against its American rival goes beyond a simple count of the contractual number of planes sold, or even the backlog of orders in the pipeline. In the future, commercial aircraft production will face the challenges of climate change, technological disruption, and new forms of geopolitical tensions.

The organizational misalignment of Boeing's strategic intent, set out in a Netflix documentary and best-selling book, *Flying Blind*, reveals how senior Boeing executives are further removed from the operational challenges of design, quality, and reliability on the shop floor. This geographic location decision creates an illusory and destructive separation between strategy, made by the board and

---

[57] See Thompson (2022). The title itself is telling – "America's Future in Aerospace Still Rides on Boeing Wings – Washington Should be Worried."

C-suite, and operational excellence, which in high reliability organizations requires employee empowerment to make critical, real-time, fail-safe choices. "Our responsibility," said President Kennedy during the Cuban missile crisis in 1962, "is not discharged by the announcement of virtuous ends" and illustrates the need for close, continuous, and unrelenting focus on strategic intent and aligning competences and capabilities to achieve zero-defect outcomes.

Almost forty years ago, two Harvard academics[58] provided a four-step model in manufacturing's strategic role, where each stage indicates the internal culture and dynamics of competitive advantage. In Stage 1 and Stage 2, the emphasis is on avoiding the negative potential of the manufacturing role in the organizational structure – mostly a reactive stance, with new equipment as the tool to maintain best industry practices, and with more executive reliance outside the production system – R&D and design, for example – to provide a competitive edge. For the most part, Boeing remains in the first two stages,[59] both in commercial aircraft and in its defense systems for the US military.

Stages 3 and 4 in this framework are manufacturing leaders with systemic collaboration with engineering and marketing, with long-term thinking and internal support to all functional areas in the firm. Stage 4 systems require "continually investing in process improvements, not only because of the resulting benefits for existing products, but because this enhances capabilities that will benefit future generation of products" (Hayes and Wheelwright, 1984, p. 402). Implicit is the adoption of more advanced manufacturing stages, with a clear C-suite understanding that manufacturing of advanced, complicated, high-reliability systems is the route to senior management jobs, or even to the C-suite.

It will take years for Boeing to recapture the firm's global reputation, other than as a large industrial aerospace manufacturer, but with little advantage by design, size, or brand. Airbus, an unexpected entrant to this technological sector, overtook Boeing in number of planes delivered, and since 2023, the gap has widened, from 611 to Boeing's 340. More vitally, Airbus now leads with its family of A320 jets, producing seventy a month compared to production of Boeing's 737 MAX at thirty-one per month, with huge consequences for monthly cash flow. Airbus's

---

[58] See Hayes and Wheelwright (1984).

[59] Boeing's quality problems seem extensive and pervasive across different models and factories and reflect a passive, complacent stance in the C-suite. The dysfunctions of manufacturing culture at Boeing are well known in the aerospace industry, including a major customer, the US Department of Defense, and its various units, including the Air Force. In 2019, years after the fatalities of the 737 MAX, the US Air Force took delivery of the KC-46 tanker jets, based on the frame of a Boeing 767 with a cockpit of a 787, only to find up to ten loose tools and debris located in various parts of the tanker plane, thus delaying training practices for a week. Such mishaps are far from a defect-free system, which is in part the fault of mechanics and quality inspectors, just when Boeing expects to cut quality inspectors by 1,000 positions in the next two years (Gates, 2019). See also Krishnamoothi, K. S. (1992).

investments in annual R&D, including a focus on net zero carbon emissions, with new collaboration, joint ventures, and alliances for alternative fuels and plane design, including gas hybrids, electric, and hydrogen, and fuel cells.

Future Boeing strategies are in place now and will determine if its past reputation as a pioneer can be refurbished. A decade from now, as shown in many sectors, China's designs for commercial aircraft can't be underestimated, in part because it has a huge internal market and strong diplomatic relations with large foreign markets like Brazil, the Continent of Africa, and Russia. Further, despite laudatory comments from Boeing's C-suite, and not a few MBA bank analysts on Wall Street, Boeing's foray in the defense and space side of its product line faces real headwinds from other American defense companies like Lockheed Martin, Northrop Grumman, General Dynamics, Raytheon, and Textron. They have won very big contracts with revenues and long-term repeat orders, and Boeing's CST-100 Starliner spacecraft, a fixed-price contract with NASA, faces technical flaws, cost overruns, and scheduling delays, just as an alternative model, the Dream Chaser – have been developed by Sierra Space, with both a version for a crew of seven and a cargo version to resupply the International Space Station – has been developed. But this future development is thwarted by a pervasive dysfunctional corporate culture, starting at Boeing's board and C-suite. And rivals like SpaceX, Virgin Galactic now provide NASA with launching options.

Boeing and Airbus experienced post-COVID high demand for planes, including from airlines upgrading their aging fleets, and from the newly privatized Air India, now owned and operated by the Tata Group. Worldwide, airline travel has almost returned to pre-COVID levels, as illustrated by Chinese demand, over 155 million before the pandemic, spending about $225 billion in foreign destinations. In 2020, China overtook the US as the largest aviation market. Sales deliveries steadily increased after 2016, from 119 planes for Boeing and 158 for Airbus, to 45 in 2019 and 178 for Airbus. For Boeing, sales deliveries of wide-bodied aircraft varied from 28 in 2016, to 136, 165, 24, 4, and 7 in the next five years. Narrow-bodied deliveries in 2016 were 91 aircraft, and have fallen every year since: 23, 27, 21, and none in 2020 and 2021, mainly as the result of the global grounding of the 737 MAX.

The steady growth for commercial planes in China is complicated by geopolitical tensions, where successive American administrations see China as a military threat. However, as a growing space and military superpower, China wants to have its own suppliers of aircraft, both commercial and military (Crane et al., 2014). Clearly, the government in Beijing has long-term development strategies, enhanced by Japan's Mitsubishi exiting from commercial aviation. Mitsubishi faced many unmet challenges, such as an underdeveloped supplier base, inexperienced certification personnel at the Japan Civil Aviation Bureau, and size design errors that don't address scope clauses for regional airlines.[60] China's main domestic OEM, COMAC (Commercial Aircraft Corporation), still needs foreign suppliers (see Appendix A4).[61]

The decision to relocate headquarters to Virginia, which in doublespeak is a questionable board decision to be close to the White House, key members of Congress, and the Department of Defense, is a strategic bet on a protracted US–China dispute, but potentially a move that would bar or limit Boeing's sales in China, a value in excess of $1.2 trillion. Both Boeing and Airbus have factories in China: Boeing's plant is located about 300 km southeast of Shanghai in Zhoushan, and is mostly dedicated to the 737, and Airbus's plant in Tianjin produces final assembly for the A-320 family, plus parts of the airframe for the A-220, with close cooperation of fifteen parts and components suppliers, producing an expected fourteen planes per month. Two new Chinese factories are planned.

In the near term, the global geopolitical environment shows new signs of pessimism, whereas globalization once brought greater integration and interdependence through trade and investments. Today, policy calls for derisking or outright decoupling, and potential outright withdrawal, lead to limited cooperation on only a select number of public policies. In fact, this strategic challenge is the real issue facing Boeing (and other American companies) on the ongoing US–China geopolitical tensions. The example of 1,000 Western companies with Japanese, European, and American companies closing their factories and outlets in Russia is a signal of decoupling with a vengeance,[62] the result of Russia's invasion of Ukraine, and the signs of a new international order in the making.[63]

Boeing's current corporate debt of about $45 billion greatly restricts its capacity to explore new technological options. The immediate consequence for Boeing's failures – at the board level, the firm's tarnished brand, and payouts for executive compensation – are measured in the billions, with $8.2 billion already earmarked for airline customer delays, court fines, and partial compensation for families of the crash victims. Other lawsuits against Boeing are under

---

[60] Scope clause inserted in agreements with pilots' unions give preference to pilots against outsourcing, as well as preference for mainland carriers from regional airlines. When airlines plan their route structures, often as a hub and spoke approach, they balance the types and size of aircraft to meet demand, but also to address the scope clause with the pilots from regional planes, compared to mainland fleets.

[61] Mitsubishi faced many unmet challenges, such as an underdeveloped supplier base, inexperienced certification personnel at the Japan Civil Aviation Bureau, and size design errors that don't address scope clauses for regional airlines.

[62] In academe, the financial media, and foreign policy think tanks, there is now an abundant and growing literature on the death of globalization, decoupling, and inshoring of supply chains and local sourcing. For background, see Black and Morrison (2021), Bateman (2022), and Witt et al. (2023).

[63] See Spence (2023) and Witt et al. (2023).

way, and in the scenario of another 737 MAX fatality, the survival of Boeing as an independent corporate entity would be in jeopardy (Thompson, 2022).

Boeing's share buyback strategy raises serious questions for corporate governance, despite some pablum comments from Warren Buffett in his 2022 annual letter that critics of share buybacks are "economic illiterates or silver-tongued demagogues." However, his firm, Berkshire Hathaway, forms part of a new feature of modern capitalism, the massive concentration of wealth in new financial intermediates, measured in trillions of US dollars – equity funds, sovereign wealth funds, venture capital funds, leveraged buy-out firms, vulture funds, and hedge funds. Their mission statements are relatively straightforward: invest in corporate shares to increase the share value. Yet shareholders of corporations rarely get a chance to approve share buybacks.

In fact, the mantra of shareholder maximization still has resonance in corporate boardrooms, and many companies still award huge executive compensation when they leave, even if the board decides to fire senior executives or the CEO for terrible misjudgments. Even Warren Buffett admits to investment errors in his choice of potential winners, including airline stocks. Some are skeptical. Roger Martin (2023), the former Dean of Rotman Business School in Toronto, puts the dilemma this way: "Everybody thinks the stock price is somehow a real thing that really reflects the company and its operations, and they're often baffled when earnings are up 20% and the stock goes down … It is simply the culmination of what all people in the capital markets observing the company imagined its future prospects to be. We know that because the S&P 500 has traded on average at 19x or 20x across its history, which means the stock prices incorporate 1x for current earnings and the other 19x times for future expectations. So, we believe that stock-based compensation provides an incentive to make the company perform better. It isn't."

The current share buyback controversy, with revised SEC disclosure rules and a higher tax on share buybacks (a boon for executives compensated with shares and a means to avoid paying taxes on dividends), will likely slow down but not impede this governance approach. It parallels the debate about ESG investing (E for environmental, S for social, and G for governance), where firms often limit disclosure for corporate activities, including cost-saving measures for product inspectors, illegal sourcing of goods from countries allowing slave labor, or producing fossil fuels, for example, coal, with no respect for the real costs to the environment and the health of workers. In fact, the lawsuits against Boeing on the faulty design of the 737 MAX and the vastly misleading statements to the regulators at FAA illustrate the weakness of disclosure practices in the modern corporation.

Boeing and its rival, Airbus, increasingly face the challenges of climate change, as the airline sector accounts for 3 percent of carbon emissions. They also face growing consumer choices for mobility, as well as new narratives of urban air mobility. Both Boeing and Airbus have made investments in new startups like Wisk Aero, and now a subsidiary of Boeing. These startups join thousands of others across the globe focusing on a net-zero emissions goal. Many airlines are partners in these new startups, which include efforts for plant-based fuel, with test flights in Japan, and flights by Airbus using fuel cells. Other efforts are sustainable aviation fuels, also called E-fuels, including battery innovation for electric aircraft. Potentially, major sources of innovation for zero-emission targets are aircraft engine makers like Rolls-Royce, Pratt & Whitney, and General Electric, which are developing new partnerships with leading universities, government labs, and some startups.

Boeing's protracted missteps, corporate myopia in the C-Suite, and a Board embracing group think may lead to a disruptive change in the commercial aviation duopoly. Production delays and longer delivery times impact the firm's biggest airline customers – Southwest, United, Ryanair, and American, for instance – reducing their revenue forecasts for passenger capacity in lucrative routes, and possibly adding to ticket price inflation. Delays and cutbacks also impact Boeing's free cash flow estimates, factory scheduling aligned with supplier deliveries, and inventory levels for certain spare parts and components. Airbus, with its own backlog of sales orders, may induce potential rivals, including COMAC in China, Mitsubishi Industries in Japan that may revive production of its commercial plane sector, and Embraer in Brazil to enter the commercial sector. There are also new venture firms like UP Partners in California, with its well funded portfolio of new startups, in all aspects of the aviation industry. Embraer's ambitions and global mindset might be the closest as a rival for Boeing's 737 family model, and a stepping stone to bigger sized models for cargo and passengers, using a suite of innovative sub-contractors for wing design, more efficient engines with less carbon emissions, and superior customer experience. Newer airlines also bring a measure of disruption with their own corporate incubators, experimenting with fuel efficiency, lighter composites, and willing to bring new partners into their corporate ecosystem.

For Boeing, these research developments require commitments to R&D, and the gap with Airbus forms a challenge to the firm's recovery plan. Boeing hasn't designed a new aircraft model for decades and still relies on basic airframes launched in the 1960s, despite regular upgrading and incorporating new technologies, some designed by Airbus. Since 2016, Airbus has focused more attention on its innovation ecosystem, both in Europe and other countries, including Silicon Valley in California. The firm's BizLab, a business incubator, an ideas factory within Airbus's diverse operations, is aligned with Airbus Ventures, a venture fund for early-stage startups, but linked to other external

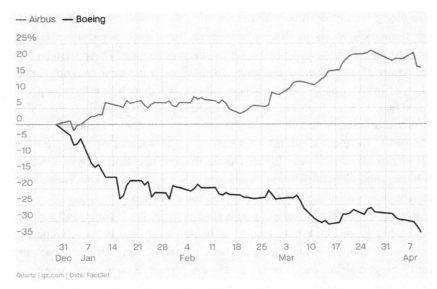

Figure 20 Aircraft manufacturer 2024 stock performance, through April 10.
Source: Morning Star (April 8, 2024).

venture funds to gain scaling quickly with potential unicorn status. New startups are linked to Airbus's immediate needs, including climate-related technologies – carbon capture and removal, civil aviation fuel, and direct air capture, alternative fuels sourcing, with related concepts of urban air mobility and service technologies like sensors, Internet of Things, and big data analytics (e.g. flight data and weather data). Core technology ventures can be independent firms, possibly listed in a stock exchange. Boeing's continued production problems across a range of models has not only delayed the delivery of planes to customers but opened a share price gap between Airbus and Boeing (see Figure 20).

The Boeing–Airbus duopoly and the differing strategies and performance outcomes illustrate a lesson for all companies who need to play the global game, whether as leaders or laggards. Geopolitical issues are a given, and so too is a requirement to redesign their business models around customers' needs and updated innovation systems at all levels of the firm. As James March (2008) noted two decades ago, with lessons for Boeing, "when firms can exploit existing skills, competences and resources, or explore new product or technological advantages, the organization becomes so competent at current alternatives that it is difficult for an adaptive process to switch to another alternative, even to one with greater potential."

Appendix

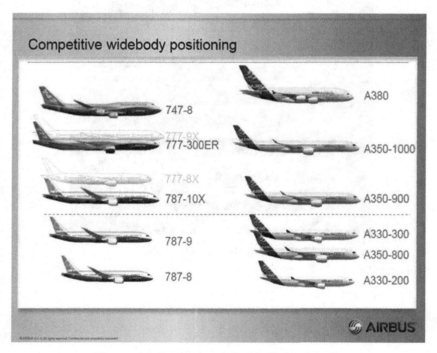

Figure A1 Comparison of wide-body aircraft.

Source: Airbus.

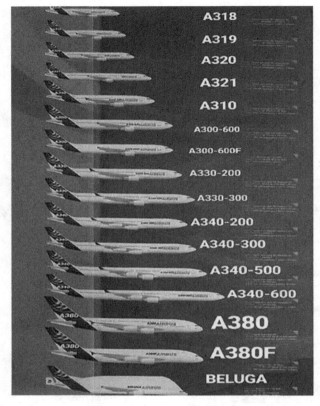

Figure A2 Airbus family of planes.

Source: Airbus.

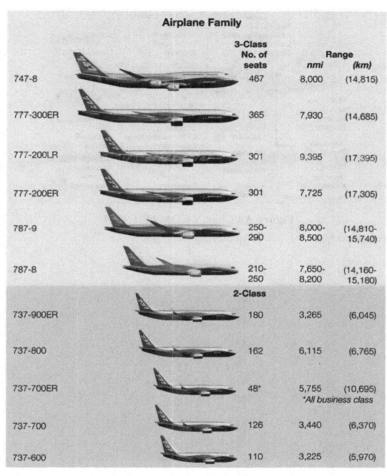

Figure A3 Boeing family of planes.

Source: Boeing.

Figure A4 China's COMAC C-919.

Source: Airinsight.

Core principles	Traditional assembly	Just-in-time
Planning & control	A push model flow	A pull model flow
Capacity planning	Large batch size	Small flexible batches
Plant design	Job shop flow	Cellular flow
Workforce	Hiring and firing based on external labor market	Stable workforce independent of short-term fluctuations of plant output
Supplier sourcing	Multiple suppliers but bias to vertical integration	Suppliers become only tier 1 & tier 2 based on benchmarks of agreed pricing, quality, and delivery
Plant layout	Designed for machines and interchangeable parts on moving assembly	Package of machines and robotics for dangerous tasks combined with craft skills
Inventory management	High buffer stocks for disruptions and defects	Inventory viewed as waste & minimized with small lots
Planning approach	Long lead times	Short lead times
Quality management	Selective inspection based on past output	A zero-defect goal based on worker QC circles
Wage system	Rates based on union-management contracts tied to seniority	Rates based on wages, group bonuses and skills accumulation
Job training	Little in-house training	Continuous training using *kaizen* principles of continuous improvement
Job tasks	Little formal training, and inflexible task assignments on assembly line	Multi-task job assignments along the assembly flow
Inspection of output	Task for plant supervisors	System by direct workers using on-the spot inspection to 'stop' cord of assembly line

Figure A5 Some comparisons of traditional manufacturing versus JIT manufacturing.

Source: Author's Analysis, based on Fujimoto (1970), McMillan (1996).

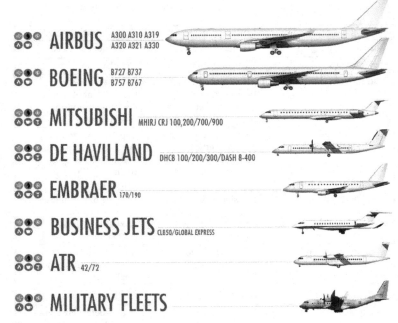

Figure A6 Variations in high-reliability aircraft manufacturers.
Source: *Aviation Week*.

YEAR	BUYBACKS	DIVIDENDS	TOTAL TO SHAREHOLDERS	BOEING'S PER-SHARE DIVIDENDS
2014	$6,001	$2,115	$8,116	$2.92
2015	$6,751	$2,490	$9,241	$3.64
2016	$7,001	$2,756	$9,757	$4.36
2017	$9,236	$3,417	$12,653	$5.68
2018	$9,000	$3,946	$12,946	$6.84
2019	$2,651	$4,630	$7,281	$8.22
Totals	$40,640	$19,354	$59,994	

Figure A7 Boeing Share Buybacks and Dividends Payouts: 2024–2019.
Source: Boeing Annual Reports.

How the MCAS system works

The Boeing 737 Max has a computer controlled stability system called MCAS

2. Horizontal stabiliser trim adjusts to correct angle if too high

1. Sensors in nose measure angle of flight

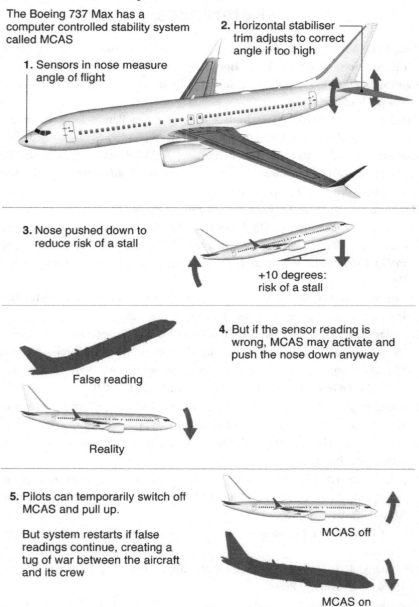

3. Nose pushed down to reduce risk of a stall

+10 degrees: risk of a stall

4. But if the sensor reading is wrong, MCAS may activate and push the nose down anyway

False reading

Reality

5. Pilots can temporarily switch off MCAS and pull up.

But system restarts if false readings continue, creating a tug of war between the aircraft and its crew

MCAS off

MCAS on

Figure A8 How the MCAS system works.

Source: BBC

References

Abegglen, James. C., & George Stalk, Jr. (1985), *Kaisha – The Japanese Corporation*. New York: Basic Books.

Agawa, H. (1969), *The Reluctant Admiral: Yamamoto and the Imperial Navy*. Tokyo: Kadasha Press.

Allerton, D. J. (2010), "The Impact of Flight Simulation in Aerospace," *Aeronautical Journal*, Vol. 114, pp. 744–756.

Amburgey, T. L., D. Kelly, and W. P. Barnett (1993), "Resetting the Clock: The Dynamics of Organizational Change and Failure," *Administrative Science Quarterly*, Vol. 38 (1), pp. 51–73.

Baldwin, C. Y., and K. B. Clark (2000), *Design Rules: The Power of Modularity*. Cambridge: The Massachusetts Institute of Technology Press.

Bateman, J. (2022), *US-China Technological "Decoupling": A Strategy and Policy Framework*, Washington, DC: Carnegie Endowment for International Peace.

Baumard, P., and W. Starbuck (2005), "Learning from Failures: Why It May Not Happen," *Long Range Planning*, Vol. 38, pp. 281–298.

Beaugency, A., M. E. Sakinç, and D. Talbot (2015), "Outsourcing of Strategic Resources and Capabilities: Opposing Choices in the Commercial Aircraft Manufacturing," *Journal of Knowledge Management*, Vol. 19 (5), pp. 912–931. DOI: https://doi.org/10.1108/JKM-01-2015-0040.

Bilstein, R. E. (1996), *The American Aerospace Industry: From Workshop to Global Enterprise*. New York: Twayne Publishers.

Black, C. (2003), *Franklin Delano Roosevelt: Champion of Freedom*. New York: Public Affairs.

Black, J. S., and A. J. Morrison (2021), "The Strategic Challenges of Decoupling: Navigating Your Company's Future in China," *Harvard Business Review*, May–June.

Brooks, P. W. (1961), *The Modern Airliner: Its Origins and Development*. London: Putnam.

Brumberg, J. L. (1999), *NASA and the Space Industry*. Baltimore: Johns Hopkins University Press.

Buergin, J., F. Belkadi, C. Hupays, et al. (2018), "A Modular-Based Approach for Just-In-Time Specification of Customer Orders in the Aircraft Manufacturing Industry," *CIRB Journal of Manufacturing Science and Technology*, Vol. 1, pp. 61–74.

Burke, R. J., G. Martin, and C. L. Cooper (Eds.) (2010), *Corporate Reputation: Managing Opportunities and Threats.* Cheltenham: Edward Elgar.

Cannon, M. D., and A. C. Edmondson (2005), "Failing to Learn and Learning to Fail (Intelligently): How Great Organizations Put Failure to Work to Innovate and Improve," *Long Range Planning*, Vol. 38, pp. 299–319.

Caves, R. E. (1962), *Air Transport and Its Regulators: An Industry Study.* Cambridge, MA: Harvard University Press.

Ciborra, C., K. Braa, A. Cordella, et al. (2000), *From Control to Drift: The Dynamics of Corporate Information Infrastructures.* Oxford: Oxford University Press.

Clinton, D. H. (1995), "(Re)learning to Fly: Russian Aviation in the Post-Soviet Era," *Journal of Air Law and Commerce*, Vol. 61 (2), pp. 467–503. https://scholar.smu.edu/jalc/vol61/iss2/6.

Cohen, K. J., and R. M. Cyert (1965), *Theory of the Firm: Resource Allocation in a Market Economy.* Englewood Cliffs, NJ: Prentice-Hall.

Copeland, D. G. C., and J. L. McKenney (1988), "Airline Reservations Systems: Lessons from History," *MIS Quarterly*, Vol. 12, pp. 353–370.

Crane, K., J. E. Luoto, S. W. Harold, et al. (2014), *The Effectiveness of China's Industrial Policies in Commercial Aviation Manufacturing.* Santa Monica, CA: RAND Corporation.

Cyert, R., and J. G. March (1963), *A Behavioral Theory of the Firm.* Englewood Cliffs, NJ: Prentice-Hall.

Dempsey, P. S., and A. R. Goetz (1992), *Airline Deregulation and Laissez Faire Mythology.* Westport, CT: Quorum Books.

de Rugy, V. (2020), "The ExIm Bank Is Still the Bank of Boeing." Barrington, MA: American Institute for Economic Research. www.aier.org/article/the-exim-bank-is-still-the-bank-of-boeing.

Douglas, G. W., and J. C. Miller III (1974). *Economic Regulation of Domestic Air Transport: Theory and Policy.* Washington, DC: The Brookings Institution.

Downer, John (2024), *Rational Accidents: Reckoning With Catastrophic Technologies, Cambridge: MIT Press.*

Driskill, M. (2019), "Boeing Forms Board Committee on Safety After Deadly MAX Crashes," *Asian Aviation.* https://asianaviation.com/boeing-forms-board-committee-on-safety.

Dunbar, R. L. M., and R. Garud (2009), "Distributed Knowledge and Indeterminate Meaning: The Case of the Columbia Shuttle Flight," *Organization Studies*, Vol. 30 (4), pp. 397–421.

Dyer, J. H., and K. Nobeoka (2000), "Creating and Managing a High Performance Knowledge-Sharing Network: The Toyota Case," *Strategic Management Journal*, Vol. 21, pp. 345–367.

Esty, B., Benjamin C., and. & P. Ghemawat (2001), "Airbus vs Boeing in Superjumbos – Credibility and Preemption," Harvard Business School Working Paper 02-061, pp. 1–41.

Fairchild, R., Richard J., and. & McGuire, S. Steven M. (2010), "The Airbus-Boeing Dispute: A Strategic Trade Theory Approach," available at SSRN: https://ssrn.com/abstract=1640536 or http://dx.doi.org/10.2139/ssrn.1640536

Fujimoto, T. (1999), *The Evolution of a Manufacturing System at Toyota*. New York: Oxford University Press.

Garicano, L., and L. Rao (2016), "Why Organizations Fail: Models and Causes," *Journal of Economic Literature*, Vol. 54 (1), pp. 137–192.

Gates, D. (2019), "Boeing Tanker Jets Grounded due to Tools and Debris Left During Manufacturing," *Seattle Times* (February 28, p. B1).

Gelles, D. (2022), *The Man Who Broke Capitalism: How Jack Welch Gutted the Heartland and Crushed the Soul of Corporate America – and How to Undo His Legacy*. New York: Simon & Schuster.

Goetz, A. R., and P. S. Dempsey (1989), "Airline Deregulation Ten Years After: Something Foul in the Air," *Journal of Air Law and Commerce*, Vol. 54, pp. 927, 927–963 https://scholar.smu.edu/jalc/vol54/iss4/3.

Goetz, A. R. (2002), "Deregulation, Competition, and Antitrust Implications in the US Airline Industry," *Journal of Transport Geography*, Vol. 10 (1), pp. 1–19.

Hamilton, S. (2021), *Air Wars: The Global Combat between Airbus and Boeing*. New York: 12S Publishing.

Hayes, R. H., and S. C. Wheelwright (1984), *Restoring Our Competitive Edge: Competing through Manufacturing*. New York: John Wiley.

Hayward, K. (1994), *The World Aerospace Industry: Collaboration and Competition*. London: Duckworth.

Hochmuth, M. S. (1974), "Aerospace," in Raymond Vernon (Ed.), *Big Business and the State: Change Relations in Western Europe*. Cambridge, MA: Harvard University Press, pp. 145–169.

Hull, K. (2014), "In Depth Look: Aircraft Production in the Former Soviet Union," *Airline Reporter* (March 28). www.airlinereporter.com/2014/03/air craft-production-in-the-former-soviet-union.

Hymer, S., and R. Rowthorne (1970), "Multinational Corporations and International Oligopoly: The Non-American Challenge," in Charles P. Kindleberger (Ed.), *The International Corporation*, Cambridge: Massachusetts Institute of Technology Press, pp. 57–91.

Johnson, M. (2010), "A New Framework for Business Models," *Harvard Business Review* (January 21), pp. 23–25.

Jordan, W. William (1970), *Airline Regulation in America: Effects and Imperfections*, Baltimore, MD: Johns Hopkins University Press.

Kasper, D. M. (1988). *Deregulation and Globalization: Liberalizing International Trade in Air Services*. New York: Ballinger Publishing Company.

Keeler, T. E. (1972), "Airline Regulation and Market Performance," *Bell Journal of Economics and Management Science*, Vol. 3 (2), pp. 399–424.

Kienstra, J. D. (2012). "Cleared for Landing: Airbus, Boeing, and the WTO Dispute over Subsidies to Large Civil Aircraft," *Northwestern Journal of International Law and Business*, Vol. 32 (3), pp. 569–606. https://scholarly commons.law.northwestern.edu/njilb/vol32/iss3/4.

Kitroeff, N., and D. Gelles (2019), "At Boeing, C.E.O.'s Stumbles Deepen a Crisis," *New York Times* (December 23). www.nytimes.com/2019/12/22/business/boeing-dennis-muilenburg-737-max.html.

Kremer, M. (1993), "The O-Ring Theory of Economic Development," *Quarterly Journal of Economics*, Vol. 108, pp. 551–575.

Krishnamoothi, K. S. (1992), *Reliability Methods for Engineers*. Milwaukee, WI: ASQ Quality Press, pp. 41–53.

Lazonick, W. (2022a), "Investing in Innovation: Confronting Predatory Value Extraction in the US Corporation," AIR Network Working Paper #22-09/01. https://theairnet.org/investing-in-innovation-confronting-predatory-value-extraction-in-the-u-s-corporation.

Lazonick, W. (2022b), "Innovation and Financialization in the Corporate Economy," in Arie Y. Lewin, Greg Linden, and David J. Teece (Eds.), *The New Enlightenment: Reshaping Capitalism and the Global Order in the 21st Century*, Cambridge: Cambridge University Press, pp. 41–53.

Lazonick, W. (2013), "The Financialization of the U.S. Corporation: What Has Been Lost, and How It Can Be Regained," *Seattle University Law Review*, Vol. 36 (2), pp. 857–909.

Lazonick, W., and M. O'Sullivan (2000), "Maximizing Shareholder Value: A New Ideology for Corporate Governance," *Economy and Society*, Vol. 29 (1), pp. 13–35.

Lombardi, M. (2008), "Seventh Heaven, 50 Years Ago, Boeing and Pan Am Revolutionized Travel with the 707," *Boeing Frontiers* (July, pp. 8–9), available at www.boeing.com/news/frontiers/archive/2008/july/i_history.pdf.

Lorange, P., and R. T. Nelson (1987), How to Organize – and Avoid – Organizational Decline. *Sloan Management Review*, Vol. 28 (3), 41–46.

MacPherson, A., and D. Pritchard (2007), "Boeing's Diffusion of Commercial Aircraft Technology to Japan: Surrendering the US Industry for Foreign Financial Support," *Journal of Labor Research* 28 (3), 301–321.

Marais, K., N. Dulac, and N. Leveson (2022), "Beyond Normal Accidents and High Reliability Organizations: The Need for an Alternative Approach to Safety in Complex Systems." Unpublished paper. Cambridge: Massachusetts Institute of Technology.

March, J. G. (2008), *Explorations in Organizations*. Stanford: Stanford University Press.

March, J. G., and Robert J. Sutton (1997), "Organizational Performance as a Dependent Variable," Organizational Science, Vol. 8, pp. 698–706.

Martin, R. (2023), "Are Today's Corporate Firms Ungovernable?" Interview in *Forbes*, April 19.

McGuire, S. (2007), "The United States, Japan and the Aerospace Industry: From Capture to Competitor?", *The Pacific Review*, Vol. 20 (3), pp. 329–350.

McMillan, C. (1985, 1996), *The Japanese Industrial System*. Berlin: deGruyter.

McMillan, C. (2022), *The Age of Consequence*. Montreal: McGill-Queen's University Press.

McMillan, C., and J. Overall (2017), "Crossing the Chasm and Over the Abyss: Perspectives on Organizational Failure," *The Academy of Management Perspectives*, Vol. 31.

Molho, D., and R. Péladin (1957), *L'Industrie Aéronautique*. Paris: Presses Universitaires de France.

Mowery, D. (1989), "The US Commercial Aircraft Industry," in David Mowery and Nathan Rosenberg (Eds.), *Technology and the Pursuit of Economic Growth*. Cambridge: Cambridge University Press, pp. 169–204.

Muellerliele, C. (2009), "Financialization Takes Off at Boeing," *Journal of Economic Geography*, Vol. 9, pp. 663–667.

Nahapiet, J., and G. Sumantra (1998), "Social Capital, Intellectual Capital, and the Organizational Advantage," *The Academy of Management Review*, Vol. 23 (2), 242–266.

Newhouse, J. (2007), *Boeing Versus Airbus: The Inside Story of the Greatest International Competition in Business*. New York: Alfred A. Knopf.

Newhouse, J. (1982), *The Sporty Game: The High-Risk Competitive Business of Making and Selling Commercial Airliners*, New York: Alfred A. Knopf.

Pattillo, D. M. (2001), *Pushing the Envelope: The American Aircraft Industry*, Ann Arbor: University of Michigan Press.

Perrow, C. (1984), *Normal Accidents: Living with High-Risk Technologies*, New York: Basic Books.

Peters, T. J., and R. H. Waterman, Jr. (1982), *In Search of Excellence – Lessons from America's Best-Run Companies*, New York: Harper & Row.

Petzinger, T. (1996), *Hard Landing: The Epic Contest for Power and Profits That Plunged the Airlines into Chaos*. New York: Three Rivers Press.

Pidgeon, N., and M. O'Leary (2000), "Man-Made Disasters: Why Technology and Organizations (Sometimes) Fail," *Safety Science*, Vol. 34, pp. 15–30.

Rae, J. B. (1968), *Climb to Greatness: The American Aircraft Industry, 1920–1960*, Cambridge: Massachusetts Institute of Technology Press.

Rappaport, A. (1998), *Creating Shareholder Value: A Guide for Managers and Investors*. New York: The Free Press.

Roberts, K. H. (1990), "Some Characteristics of Highly Reliability Organizations," *Organizational Science*, Vol. 1 (2), pp. 160–177.

Robison, P. (2019), "Boeing's 737 Max Software Outsourced to $9-an-Hour Engineers." *Bloomberg*. (June 29). www.bloomberg.com/news/articles/2019-06-28/boeing-s-737-max-software-out-sourced-to-9-an-hour-engineers

Robison, P. (2021), "A Behind the Scenes Look at Boeing's Shifting Leadership landscape – and Its Profound Effects," *Seattle Times* (December 12).

Schwab, A., and W. H. Starbuck (2016), "Collegial 'Nests' Can Foster Critical Thinking. Innovative Ideas and Scientific Progress," *Strategic Organization*, Vol. 4, pp. 161–177.

Sell, T. M. (2001), *Wings of Power: Boeing and the Politics of Growth in the Northwest*, Seattle: University of Washington Press.

Serling, R. (1992), *Legend & Legacy: The Story of Boeing and Its People*. New York: St. Martin's Press.

Sheppard, J. P., and S. D. Chowdhury (2005), "Riding the Wrong Wave: Organizational Failure as a Failed Turnaround," *Long Range Planning*, Vol. 38, pp. 239–260.

Shingo, S. (1989), *A Study of the Toyota Production System*, Portland: Productivity Press.

Simonson, G. R. (1968), *The History of the American Aircraft Industry*. Cambridge: Massachusetts Institute of Technology Press.

Spaeth, A. (2021), "Emirates President Lashes Boeing for Organizational Problems," *Airline Ratings* (September 21).

Spence, M. (2023), "Destructive Decoupling," *Project Syndicate* (March 30).

Starbuck, W. H., and B. Hedberg (2001), "How Organizations Learn from Success and Failure," in M. Dierkes, A. Berthoin, J. C. Antal, and I. Nonaka (Eds.), *The Handbook of Organizational Learning and Knowledge*. Oxford: Oxford University Press.

Stekler, H. O. (1965), *The Structure and Performance of the Aerospace Industry.* Berkeley: University of California Press.

Stigler, G. J. (1971), "The Theory of Economic Regulation," *The Bell Journal of Economics and Management Science*, Vol. 2 (Spring), pp. 3–21.

Swann, D. (1972), *The Economics of the Common Market*, Harmondsworth: Penguin.

Takeuchi, H., E. Osono, and N. Shimizu (2008), "The Contradictions That Drive Toyota's Success," *Harvard Business Review* (June 1).

Teece, D. J. (2010), "Business Models, Business Strategy and Innovation," *Long Range Planning*, Vol. 43, pp. 172–194.

Thompson, L. (2022), "America's Future in Aerospace Still Rides on Boeing Wings. Washington Should be Worried," *Forbes (*April 29).

Useem, J. (2019), "The Long-Forgotten Flight That Sent Boeing Off Course: A Company Once Driven by Engineers Became Driven by Finance," *The Atlantic* (September 20).

Vander Meulen, J. (1991), *The Politics of Aircraft: Building an American Military Industry.* Lawrence: University Press of Kansas.

Vartabedian, R. (1996), "Boeing to Acquire Douglas, Creating Aerospace Behemoth," *Los Angeles Times* (December 16).

Vaughan, D. (1996), *The Challenger Launch Decision: Risky Technology, Culture, and Deviance at NASA.* Chicago: University of Chicago Press.

Viardot, E. (2022), *Airbus 2022: Smooth Skies Ahead?* Case Study, Skema Business School.

Waldmeir, P. (2019), "Boeing Suppliers Face Impact of the Max Crisis," *Financial Times* (May 3).

Welch, J. (2021), "Will Boeing Soar Again? Navigating a Corporate Recovery Process," *The Journal of Business Strategy*, Vol. 42 (5), pp. 323–331.

Wills, Gordon (1969), *Technological Forecasting and Social Change.* London: Penguin.

Winston, C., and S. A. Morrison (2001). *The Evolution of the Airline Industry.* Washington: The Brookings Institution.

Witt, M. A., A. Y. Lewin, P. P. Li., and A. Gaur (2023), "Decoupling in International Business: Evidence, Drivers, Impact, and Implications for IB Research," *Journal of World Business*, Vol. 58, pp. 1–10.

Womack, J. P., D. T. Jones, and D. Roos (1990), *The Machine That Changed the World: The Story of Lean Production – Toyota's Secret Weapon in the Global Car Wars That Is Now Revolutionizing World Industry.* New York: Free Press.

Zeng, Liyu and P. Luk (2020), "Examining Share Repurchasing and the S&P Buyback Indices in the U.S. Market," *S&P Research*, New York: SP Global.

Acknowledgments

In preparing and writing this Element, I wish to acknowledge the help and guidance of Arie Y. Lewin, Professor Emeritus of Strategy and International Business at Duke University and coeditor, with Till Talaulicar, of the Cambridge Elements Series Reinventing Capitalism. I also wish to acknowledge and thank two anonymous external reviewers, as well as George Stalk, Ian McDougall, and Eric Viadot (author of a teaching case on Airbus) for their detailed comments on earlier drafts of the manuscript. I also acknowledge the great assistance of Krithika Shivakumar for her help with figures and edits in text. Finally, I take full responsibility for any errors of omission or commission.

Cambridge Elements ≡

Reinventing Capitalism

Arie Y. Lewin

Duke University

Arie Y. Lewin is Professor Emeritus of Strategy and International Business at Duke University, Fuqua School of Business. He is an Elected Fellow of the Academy of International Business and a Recipient of the Academy of Management inaugural Joanne Martin Trailblazer Award. Previously, he was Editor-in-Chief of *Management and Organization Review* (2015–2021) and the *Journal of International Business Studies* (2000–2007), founding Editor-in-Chief of Organization Science (1989–2007), and Convener of Organization Science Winter Conference (1990–2012). His research centers on studies of organizations' adaptation as co-evolutionary systems, the emergence of new organizational forms, and adaptive capabilities of innovating and imitating organizations. His current research focuses on de-globalization and decoupling, the Fourth Industrial Revolution, and the renewal of capitalism.

Till Talaulicar

University of Erfurt

Till Talaulicar holds the Chair of Organization and Management at the University of Erfurt where he is also the Dean of the Faculty of Economics, Law and Social Sciences. His main research expertise is in the areas of corporate governance and the responsibilities of the corporate sector in modern societies. Professor Talaulicar is Editor-in-Chief of *Corporate Governance: An International Review*, Senior Editor of Management and Organization Review and serves on the Editorial Board of Organization Science. Moreover, he has been Founding Member and Chairperson of the Board of the International Corporate Governance Society (2014–2020).

Editorial Advisory Board

About the Series

This series seeks to feature explorations about the crisis of legitimacy facing capitalism today, including the increasing income and wealth gap, the decline of the middle class, threats to employment due to globalization and digitalization, undermined trust in institutions, discrimination against minorities, global poverty and pollution. Being grounded in a business and management perspective, the series incorporates contributions from multiple disciplines on the causes of the current crisis and potential solutions to renew capitalism.

Panmure House is the final and only remaining home of Adam Smith, Scottish philosopher and 'Father of modern economics.' Smith occupied the House between 1778 and 1790, during which time he completed the final editions of his master works: The Theory of Moral Sentiments and The Wealth of Nations. Other great luminaries and thinkers of the Scottish Enlightenment visited Smith regularly at the House across this period. Their mission is to provide a world-class twenty-first-century centre for social and economic debate and research, convening in the name of Adam Smith to effect positive change and forge global, future-focussed networks.

ADAM SMITH
PANMURE
HOUSE

Printed in the United States
by Baker & Taylor Publisher Services